COLORFUL COOKING

Healthy and Fun Recipes That Kids Can Make

Jacque Wick

© 2014 Jacque Wick

All rights reserved.

No part of this book may be reproduced in any form whatsoever, whether by graphic, visual, electronic, film, microfilm, tape recording, or any other means, without prior written permission of the publisher, except in the case of brief passages embodied in critical reviews and articles.

ISBN: 978-1-4621-1520-4

Published by Front Table Books, an imprint of Cedar Fort, Inc.
2373 W. 700 S., Springville, UT, 84663
Distributed by Cedar Fort, Inc., www.cedarfort.com

Library of Congress Cataloging-in-Publication Data

  Wick, Jacque, 1957-
  Colorful cooking / Jacque Wick.
    pages cm
  Includes index.
  ISBN 978-1-4621-1520-4 (acid-free paper)
  1. Cooking--Juvenile literature. 2. Color of food--Juvenile literature. I. Title.
  TX652.5.W5325 2014
  641.5'622--dc23

                        2014024253

Cover and page design by Bekah Claussen
Cover design © 2014 by Lyle Mortimer
Edited by Rachel Munk

PW Perspective font designed by Peax Web Design

Printed in China

10 9 8 7 6 5 4 3 2 1

I would like to dedicate this book to a song. It may be unusual for a cookbook, but this is the song that stayed with me as I wrote this book. It goes like this:

HAVE I DONE ANY GOOD IN THE WORLD TODAY?
HAVE I HELPED ANYONE IN NEED?

Teaching children about food and cooking will give them tools for a lifetime of necessary skills and happy moments. This indeed is doing something "good in the world."

This became my dedication song when I came across a video of Alex Boye and Carmen Rasmusen performing their own version of this song. This video and rendition of the song really touched my heart.

In a similar way, this book takes simple recipes and makes them accessible to children, who can then make the recipes their own while still eating healthy and whole foods. For many tastes and desires, I have added extra ways to make it their own. As the song continues:

DOING GOOD IS A PLEASURE,
A JOY BEYOND MEASURE,
A BLESSING OF DUTY AND LOVE.

I hope that this book will bring blessings and good to those who use it to do good, and to teach good and healthy habits.

CONTENTS

INTRODUCTION VI

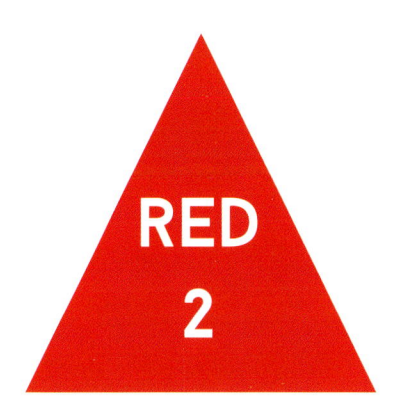

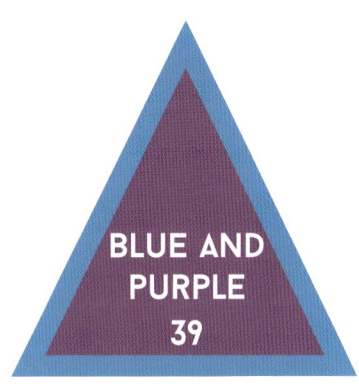

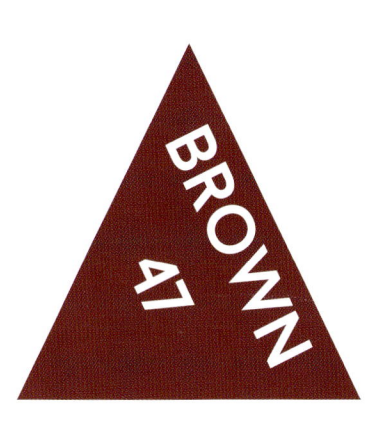

- RED 2
- ORANGE 12
- YELLOW 23
- GREEN 31
- BLUE AND PURPLE 39
- BROWN 47
- COLORFUL FOODS 56

INDEX 65
ACKNOWLEDGMENTS 66
ABOUT THE AUTHOR 66
CHILD CHEFS 68

Contents o V

Introduction

Coloring your plate with your food sounds fun to kids and adults. Children love to learn about natural colors in nature. The familiar question "why is the sky blue?" can now be "why are blueberries blue?" Here is the answer. The pigment of colors you see in plants and natural foods is the result of a function called photosynthesis. Photosynthesis means that plants take light from the sun and turn it into energy. Each plant reflects light differently because of its unique characteristics. Because each plant absorbs and reflects sunlight differently, each plant has its own unique energy pattern. These energy patterns, or the way sunlight reflects off of plants, give each plant its own color. Each plant also has its own nutrients, which we can see and understand because of the plant's color. Behavioral scientists tell us that we eat with our eyes before food ever gets to our mouth, so it is important to know which nutrients are represented in our food by which colors.

ORANGE AND GREEN AND IN-BETWEEN
What does the color of my food tell me?

The colors of our food and the different nutrition they give our bodies can be a reminder to eat a variety of colors. There are so many kinds of nutrition in each color of food. This is because many times, one food can have more than one pigment of color. To keep it simple, it's best to just explain to children the concept that colors in foods mean different pigments, and that each pigment represents a nutrient that performs an important task in our bodies, keeping us healthy.

ORANGE pigments of color in our fruits and vegetables are called carotenes. The brighter the orange, the more carotenes are in the food. There are many carotenes in carrots, sweet potatoes, and cantaloupe. One of those carotenes is called beta-carotene. Our bodies turn beta-carotene into vitamin A after we eat it. Beta-carotene is needed for healthy eyes and skin, and can also help our bodies fight off germs.

YELLOW fruits and vegetables have a lot of vitamin C, which helps us fight colds and germs. It also helps our bodies heal from cuts and bruises. Fruits like lemons have lots of vitamin C. Many foods have pigments of more than one color, like oranges. Oranges are a lighter shade of orange than pumpkins because they carry both orange and yellow pigments.

RED fruits and vegetables contain lycopene. Lycopene attacks harmful particles in our bodies that could become diseases, like cancer. Natural red foods have a lot of vitamin C, like many yellow foods, and have beta-carotene, just like orange foods. Darker red foods, like cherries, contain a blue pigment called anthocyanin. This dark red food is great for your heart and other organs in your body.

GREEN vegetables carry a pigment called chlorophyll. Chlorophyll gives plants their green color and helps capture sunlight and turn it into energy for the plant. We need to eat lots of green vegetables to give us energy and to have strong bodies. Green vegetables are full of vitamin K, an important vitamin for our bodies. It works with calcium and minerals to make our bones strong.

BLUE, PURPLE, and some RED foods carry a pigment called anthocyanin. Foods carrying anthocyanin belong to a group called flavonoids, which help protect your heart and other important organs. They are also good for brain health—helping you to think properly and remember things. They are considered super foods.

WHITE fruits and vegetables are great for your body. A group of pigments called anthoxanthins gives these foods their white to yellow color and contains antioxidants, which keep your body in balance and in working order. They do this by helping to remove some of the harmful particles that get into your body. When we get sick, one of the best foods to eat is a soup with lots of onion and garlic.

vi o Wick

BROWN rice, meat, and many varieties of beans contain vitamin B, which is good for your brain and mental health. When your brain is working well, you can think clearly and feel fewer nervous, anxious feelings. Meat also has iron, which promotes good blood health. Blood seems scary to children when they have a cut or scrape, but we need to help them understand that our blood is good. It carries the oxygen we breathe to all the cells in our body.

Minerals and trace minerals are also found in all these colorful food groups. Each color of food, and its accompanying nutrients, has a role and purpose in keeping our bodies and brains healthy.

FOOD GROUPS
Eating a Variety of Foods Daily

1. Grains
2. Fruits and Vegetables
3. Protein
4. Dairy
5. Oils

The most common **GRAINS** are wheat, rice, and oats. Many children will recognize grains as bread, cereal, and pasta. Whole-grain flour and brown rice are more nutritious than white flour and rice, because whole grains contain minerals and vitamins for our health. White flour has less nutrition and is used most in desserts. This is to give the baked desserts more of a smooth texture. Remember to use whole grain foods as much as possible. They will have the word "whole" on the food package. Some new plants that have become popular to use, similar to grain, are buckwheat and quinoa.

FRUITS AND VEGETABLES are the most commonly known colorful foods, from purple grapes and green lettuce to orange carrots and red tomatoes. Using these, you can create visually appealing recipes, along with good balanced nutrition. At some specialty markets you can even find edible flowers to use as food accents.

The **DAIRY** food group includes milk, cheese, and yogurt. These have lots of calcium, magnesium, and vitamin D for strong bones and healthy teeth. Food like ice cream and pudding are also in the dairy food group, as they are made with milk. Our bodies make vitamin D through a process of sunlight on our skin. You may use a vitamin D supplement if your child is not exposed to enough sunlight, along with adding vitamin D-rich foods to their diet.

The **PROTEIN** group includes peas, beans, eggs, nuts, seeds, fish, meat, and some dairy. Protein helps your body create muscle. It also gives you quick energy—that's why eggs are a popular protein to start the day. Protein should be eaten throughout the day for maximum energy levels. Protein-rich foods range from brown to white in this food group. A popular protein for kids is peanut butter. Kids will recognize hamburgers, hotdogs, and chicken as sources of protein.

OIL is a common part of cooking and eating. Some oils are good for you. Plant oils have some of the same omega oils that fish have. Cooking with coconut oil or a good olive oil can have great health benefits, like preventing your skin and hair from drying out. Butter tastes great and has minimal processing. If you visit a farm, you and your children may be able to see how to make butter from fresh cow's milk.

HERBS are not a food group, but they should be mentioned. Herbs can come in many colors and can be useful for medicinal purposes, as well as for food preparation. Explain to your children that we only use a small amount of herbs because they have strong tastes. It is becoming popular for live herb plants, like basil and mint, to be sold in grocery markets. Many children love having "pet" herb plants, although adults will most likely be doing the watering.

NON-FOOD GROUPS: Some foods are not considered a part of any one food group. These foods are great for occasional fun treats. Chocolate is one traditional example. I have seen recent studies of dark chocolate showing some health benefits; but sadly, chocolate has not yet been accepted into any of the food groups.

GOOD HABITS AND KITCHEN SAFETY

I advise that parents and grandparents focus more on safety rules than on messes. If children get too many frowns in the kitchen, they may not think cooking is fun, so it's important to be patient with them as they make a few messes. When children get used to cooking, you can teach them clean according to their age and maturity.

Sensible kitchen rules for adults to use and teach their children:

1. Stay close to the kitchen when cooking on a stove top or in an oven. Make sure to set timers.
2. Make sure the area around the stove is clear and keep your sleeves rolled up.
3. Pot handles should be turned inward toward the stove, so that pots are less likely to be knocked over.
4. Always use oven mitts when something is hot, including pot handles. Just because they are coated, does not mean they are cool enough for little hands.
5. Make sure the stove and oven are turned off when you are finished cooking.
6. First Aid: Even the best of us can get a burn or cut now and then. Know what to do so you don't panic if an accident happens.
7. Young cooks should use knives that are older and more dull. Let them know which ones they may use. Keep sharp knives and dangerous kitchen tools out of reach.
8. When you teach about cooking on a stove top, show children parts of the pan that will be hot. Show them the handle. Point out that they can use hot pads when they need to protect themselves from something hot.

SENSIBLE HABITS FOR CHILDREN

1. Tell an adult you will be cooking. Always ask for help when needed. Let an adult cook with you as you use knives or a stove, microwave, or oven.
2. Read the complete recipe before you start.
3. Gather all the ingredients and kitchen tools before you start cooking.
4. Wash your hands before you begin.
5. Enjoy yourself. Don't worry about mistakes. Making mistakes is part of learning.

MAKING A LIST, CHECKING IT TWICE
Letting Kids Help as They Learn

To market we go, to market we go; teach me what I need to know and grow.

The supermarket is like a field trip for young kids. Sometimes life gets so fast that we forget to slow down and use the opportunities placed right in front of us. If Mom and Dad are excited about food shopping, their excitement rubs off on the children. It's interesting to see which aisles have fruit and which have vegetables. Grocery shopping is a wonderful teaching tool that the parents are usually unaware of. If you stop and think, you can come up with many great ideas to make shopping fun and teachable.

SOME THINGS CHILDREN CAN LEARN IN THE KITCHEN AND AT THE GROCERY STORE

1. Math: How much does the food weigh? The fruit and produce is priced by weight. Another way to learn about numbers is by teaching them the cost of food. As a teacher, I know that the more children learn about money, the easier it is to teach them decimals and fractions later.

2. Science: Children can discover how food changes. Liquids can be frozen and become solids. As you heat or boil liquids such as water, you can see that they turn to vapor. The boiling liquid becomes lower in the pan as it evaporates in the air. Even learning how food is made can be a science lesson. Take your children to a working farm. Sometimes children who eat selectively decide that they like a food if they pick it from a farm. I knew one child that didn't like peaches until we went to a peach grove and picked the peaches ourselves.

3. Reading: Kids can read signs or labels. At first, kids will learn simple words or the letters of the alphabet. They can see the word *apple*, or at least the letter *A* in the sign above the apples in the produce isles. You can ask them, "Where is the letter A?"

4. Writing: Your child can help you write a list of foods you need to buy for a recipe. Don't worry about messy writing. If they cannot write yet, they can draw a picture of the food: If the recipe needs a carrot, they can draw a carrot.

5. Imagination: Younger children can play games and activities related to cooking and food to build creativity and imagination. (For example: "I'm thinking of a red fruit. What is it?")

EXPERIMENTING WITH NEW HEALTHY SNACKS

Making just a few changes at a time is the best way to introduce new foods to children. Try substituting dehydrated fruit for candy, or baked veggie chips for potato chips. There are more nutritious ways to snack using fruits and vegetables that your children can come to love. It only takes a few changes to bring some fun, healthy alternatives to your kitchen.

COOKING BASICS FOR KIDS

USING THE MICROWAVE: Make sure you have supervision at the beginning. You need to use microwave-safe bowls and cups. Plastic, glass, and some serving dishes may be used. Parents and grandparents will know which ones are microwave safe. Never put metal or aluminum foil in the microwave. Never put a metal utensil, like a spoon, in the microwave. These will cause the microwave to spark and maybe even break.

MIXING INGREDIENTS IN A BOWL: Be sure the bowl is large enough or the ingredients may spill over the sides. Use a large spoon or spatula for mixing. While mixing, scrape the ingredients from the side of the bowl and mix them around and around. If the bowl moves around while mixing, a sibling or adult can hold it for you.

CRACKING AN EGG: Take an egg and tap it lightly on the edge of the bowl with one hand. You will see gooey egg coming out of the bottom. Put the egg over the bowl. While holding on to the egg with both hands, gently pull it apart from the bottom with your two thumbs. This takes practice. If you are a beginner, you may need to crack the egg over a separate bowl and then pour it into the container for the recipe. Always ask grown-ups if you can crack the eggs when they are cooking so that you can practice.

CUTTING FRESH GARLIC: Garlic cloves need to be broken away from the larger garlic head. Lay the clove down on the cutting board. Cut the root off the garlic glove. Take a fork and push on the clove with the bottom of the fork until you smash the clove. You may hear it make a cracking noise. Peel the shell off the clove. You can now cut the garlic clove into smaller pieces.

CUTTING ONIONS: Begin by cutting the root off. This allows you to pull the outside layer off easily. Cut the onion into two pieces. Lay each piece on the cutting board flat-side down. Doing this keeps the onion from slipping while you cut. Cut the onion into slices. Recipes that need chopped or diced onions need the onion cut into smaller pieces.

ONIONS CAN MAKE YOU CRY. Your eyes may water and sting if it's an onion with a strong flavor. An old trick is to put half of a piece of bread between your lips while you cut. The bread absorbs the vapors released from the onion before they reach your eyes.

x o Wick

SHOPPING BASICS TO HAVE ON HAND

LEMONS OR LIMES: They taste good squeezed into drinks and on desserts, rice, and snacks. They also detox germs in food and drinks.

TORTILLAS AND PITA BREAD: These are useful for filling up and making fast easy meals.

BUTTER AND COCONUT OIL: It is not wise to eat lots of butter, but new research has shown it's better than other comparable options, like margarine. Coconut Oil is a very good product. I like the taste and substitute it for butter about half the time.

YOGURT: This is great for breakfast, a snack, or cooking. I like to buy the large containers and add my own fruit and sweetener. I save money and get what I want.

CINNAMON: This spice is good to have in the cupboard for many recipes, or just to put on your morning cereal. It goes hand in hand with vanilla for desserts.

BLUE AGAVE: This is a sweetener that is slowly absorbed in the body preventing sugar ups and downs. It has a good taste to it. Most grocery stores have many choices of sweeteners including agave. Experimenting with other natural sweeteners can be fun. I still enjoy cane sugar for some of my cooking needs.

VANILLA (REAL EXTRACT): It is one of my favorite flavors. I only use real vanilla.

FRESH FRUIT AND VEGETABLES: Buy weekly. Try to find a farmers market to save on costs.

CANNED AND FROZEN FRUIT AND VEGETABLES: These are great to have as backup when you cannot get fresh.

ALMOND MILK: This type of non-dairy milk has lots of calcium and minerals. It also has a pleasant taste.

QUINOA: Quinoa looks like brown rice. It has a good taste, which is making this a popular food. Quinoa has a great balance of vitamins. It also has a good amount of protein and will raise energy levels. It can be cooked easily in water in the microwave and you are able to keep cooked quinoa in the fridge for about six days.

REMEMBER that healthy changes can take time. Try some healthy new snacks like dried fruit instead of candy. Try baked veggie chips instead of potato chips.

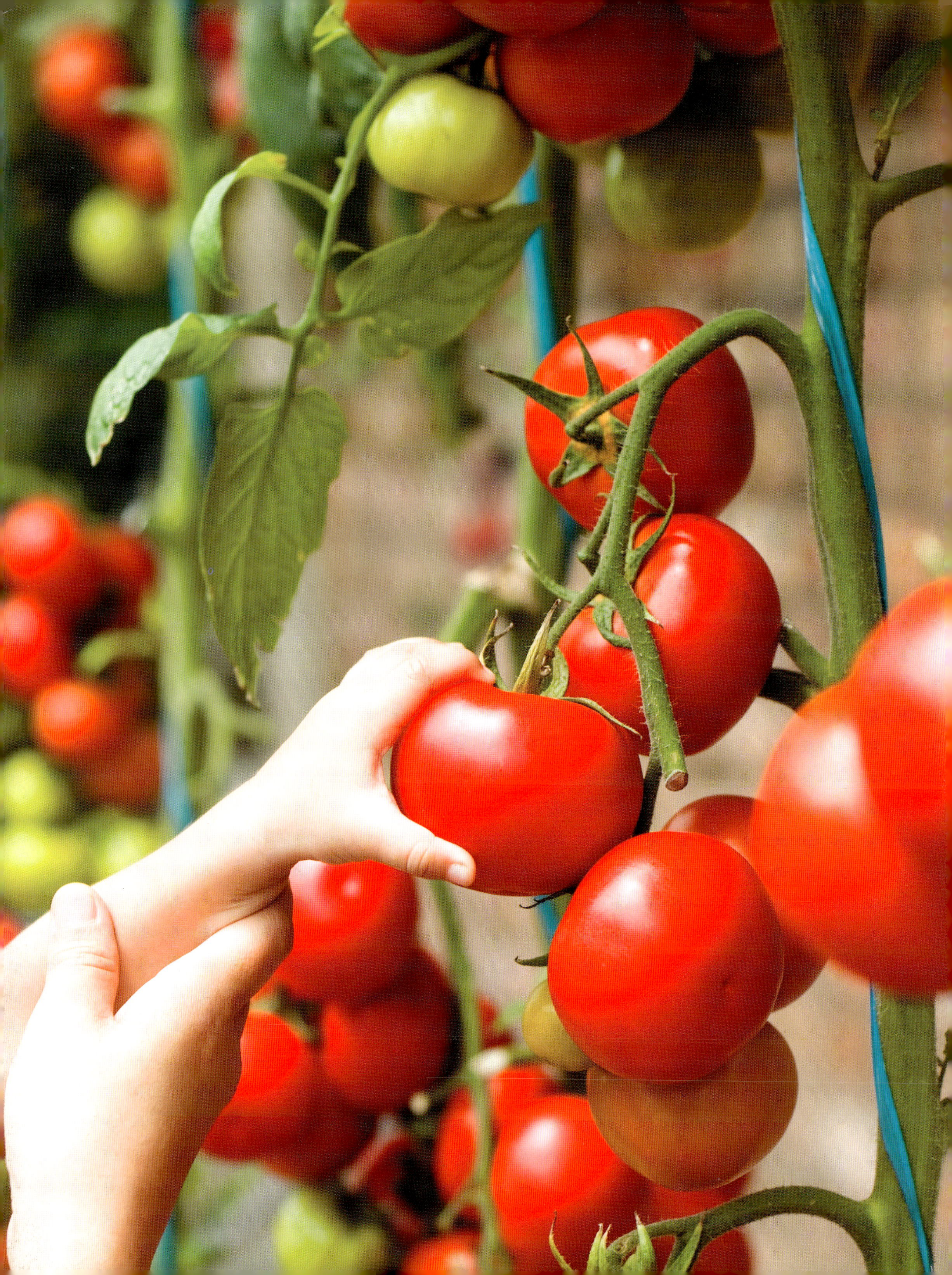

RED

Strawberry Shortcake Crepes
(serves 5)

KITCHEN TOOLS

medium bowl
cutting board
butter knife
spoon
plate
measuring spoons

INGREDIENTS

20 strawberries
4 Tbsp. cane sugar or just a bit less agave
½ pkg. ready-made crepes
⅛ cup vanilla yogurt

FOOD GROUPS

Grain	crepe
Fruit	strawberries
Dairy	yogurt

2 o Wick

DIRECTIONS

1. Rinse the strawberries.
2. Cut off and throw away the green stems. Cut the strawberries into small bits.
3. Put the strawberries in a bowl. Add the sugar or agave.
4. Put a crepe on a plate. Add the strawberry mixture to the crepe. Add yogurt.
5. Fold one side of the crepe toward the middle of crepe. Fold the other side on top.
6. Decorate the top with more strawberries.

WHAT ELSE CAN YOU DO?

Use agave instead of cane sugar.

Use other berries instead of strawberries.

Substitute cream cheese for half of the yogurt.

Parents or grandparents can pre-make crepes instead of buying store-bought.

Level of difficulty: **EASY**
(adult supervision for cutting)

1

2

3

4

5

1

2

3

4

5

Fiesta Salsa

(serves 4)

DIRECTIONS

1. Peel off the outside layer of the tomatillos. (Sometimes the outer layer sticks to the fruit inside. Just pull harder to get it off.)
2. Wash the tomatillos under running water in the sink. (Sometimes tomatillos look like they have dirt on them. This is not actually dirt, but part of the plant. It's easy to clean and isn't harmful.)
3. Cut the ingredients so they fit in the food processor or blender.
4. Squeeze the lemon juice into the food processor or blender.
5. Squeeze the orange juice into the food processor or blender.
6. Turn on the food processor to blend the ingredients (count to 5 slowly). If you are using a blender, count to 3. Check to see if the ingredients have blended enough. Some people like thick salsa, and some like it more thin.
7. When the salsa is ready, turn off the processor or blender and pour the salsa into a bowl. Serve with tortilla chips or veggie chips.

WHAT CAN GO WRONG?

See Cooking Basics for Kids on page ix for instructions on cutting onion and garlic. I left jalapeños out of the salsa because it can be too spicy for some children. If you add ½ of a jalapeño, be sure to have a older sibling or adult cut it for you.

WHAT ELSE CAN YOU DO?

You can substitute garlic salt for the garlic and salt.

Level of difficulty: MEDIUM
(adult supervision for food processor and cutting onion and garlic)

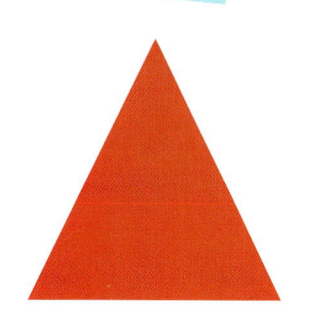

KITCHEN TOOLS

food processor or blender
cutting board
dull knife
measuring spoons

INGREDIENTS

6 tomatillos
3 large tomatoes
1 garlic clove
2 Tbsp. chopped onion
8 sprigs cilantro
1 tsp. salt
2 tsp. lime or lemon juice
1 Tbsp. orange juice
chips

FOOD GROUPS

Fruits	lemon juice
	orange juice
	tomatillos
Vegetables	tomatoes
	onion
	garlic

Red o 5

1

2

3

4

Chocolate Strawberry Dips
(serves 5)

DIRECTIONS

1. Rinse the strawberries in a strainer under tap water. Let them dry well so the chocolate will stick.
2. Break apart the chocolate and put it in a microwave-safe bowl. (If you are using Baker's Dipping Chocolate, just pull off the top of the container and put it in the microwave.)
3. Cook in the microwave for about 30 seconds. If the chocolate needs to melt more, stir it with a spoon, and then let it cook for 20 more seconds. Take it out carefully. The container may be hot.
4. Make sure the strawberries are dry so the chocolate will stick well. Dip the strawberries into the melted chocolate by holding them by their stems.
5. Place the dipped strawberries on wax paper. Let cool for 10 minutes.

WHAT ELSE YOU CAN DO?

You can dip sliced apple slices. Try covering the dipped strawberries with sprinkles, shredded coconut, or mini chocolate chips..

Level of difficulty: **EASY**
(adult supervision for microwave)

KITCHEN TOOLS

strainer
microwave-safe bowl
microwave
wax paper

INGREDIENTS

15 strawberries
melting chocolate (I like Baker's Dipping Chocolate)

FOOD GROUPS

Fruit | strawberries

Red o 7

KITCHEN TOOLS

blender
knife
cutting board
tall drinking glasses

INGREDIENTS

5 strawberries
1 cup mango
1/8 cup sugar or 2 Tbsp. agave
1½ cups plain sparkling natural mineral water or soda water
ice

FOOD GROUPS

Fruit | mango, strawberries

8 o Wick

Mango Berry Seltzer
(serves 2)

DIRECTIONS

1. Rinse off the strawberries. Cut the green stems off. Cut the strawberries smaller if you need to for your blender.
2. Have a parent help you cut the mango. Watch out for the big seed in the center. Do not use the skin of the mango.
3. Add the fruit to a blender. Squeeze the juice of 1 orange into the blender.
4. Add 1½ cups of sparkling mineral water or soda water. Add the sugar and agave to the blender. Turn on the blender.
5. Blend well for about 40 seconds. Count to 40 slowly, and then turn off the blender.
6. Add ice to two glasses.
7. Pour the mixture from the blender into the glasses.
8. Drink up!

WHAT TO KNOW?

Cutting up a mango takes practice for parents and grandparents. The mango has a big seed in the center. Cut off each end before half way to avoid the seed. Take the flesh out of the 2 pieces cut off. The center part should be cut careful to get the flesh out.

Level of difficulty: MEDIUM
(adult supervision for cutting fruit)

1

2

3

4

5

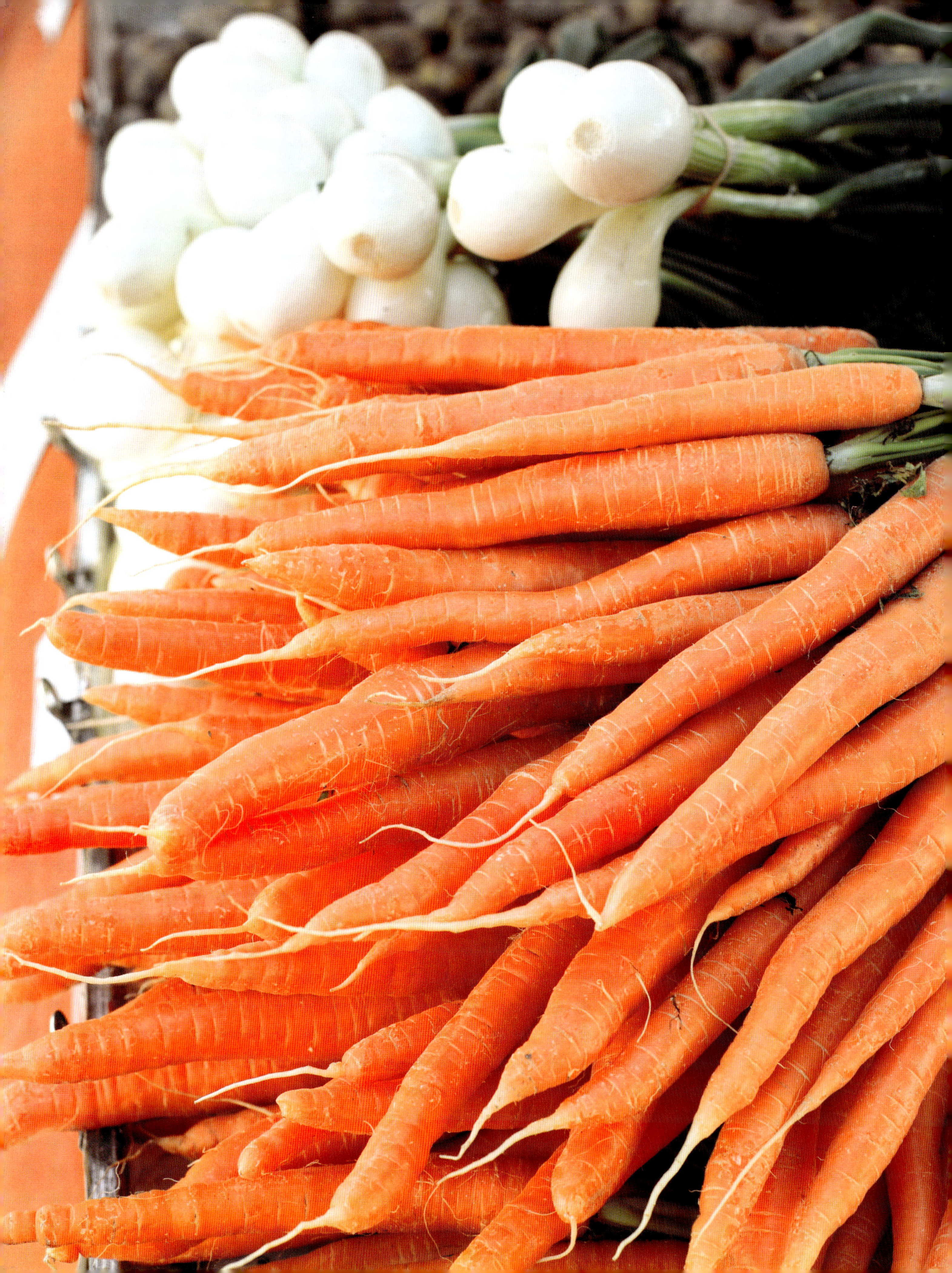

ORANGE

Cinnamon Sweet Potato Fries
(serves 4)

KITCHEN TOOLS

sharp knife (for adult to cut potatoes—never let children have a sharp knife)
cutting board
baking pan
baking rack (keeps fries off pan so they are more crispy)

INGREDIENTS

2 large sweet potatoes
2 tsp. olive oil
1 tsp. cinnamon
½ tsp. salt
2 tsp. sugar

FOOD GROUPS

Vegetables | sweet potatoes

12 o Wick

DIRECTIONS

1. Preheat the oven to 425 degrees.
2. Rinse the potatoes under water. Scrub well with your fingers or a veggie brush.
3. On cutting board, cut the sweet potatoes into fry-size pieces (this step must be done by an adult).
4. Add the sweet potatoes fries to a bowl.
5. Add the cinnamon, salt, and sugar.
6. Stir the sweet potatoes in the bowl until the pieces are covered with cinnamon sugar.
7. Place the sweet potatoes in a single formation on the wire rack with a cookie sheet underneath. (Foil can be placed on cookie sheet to catch drips.)
8. Place in the oven for 25–30 minutes. (If you didn't use a rack, turn over fries after cooking for 15 minutes to make sure they cook evenly.)
9. Take out of the oven carefully. Let an adult supervise. Leave the fries for about 10 minutes to cool off.

WHAT ELSE CAN YOU DO?

You can add baby carrots sliced in 4 pieces along with the sweet potatoes.

Instead of cinnamon and sugar, use 2 teaspoons salt. Fry sauce is good for plain fries. Fry sauce: ⅓ cup ketchup and ⅔ cup mayonnaise.

You can buy pre-cut frozen sweet potato fries at most grocery stores. Add them to sugar/cinnamon and follow directions for cooking.

Level of difficulty: **HARD**
(adult supervision of oven & adult to cut sweet potatoes)

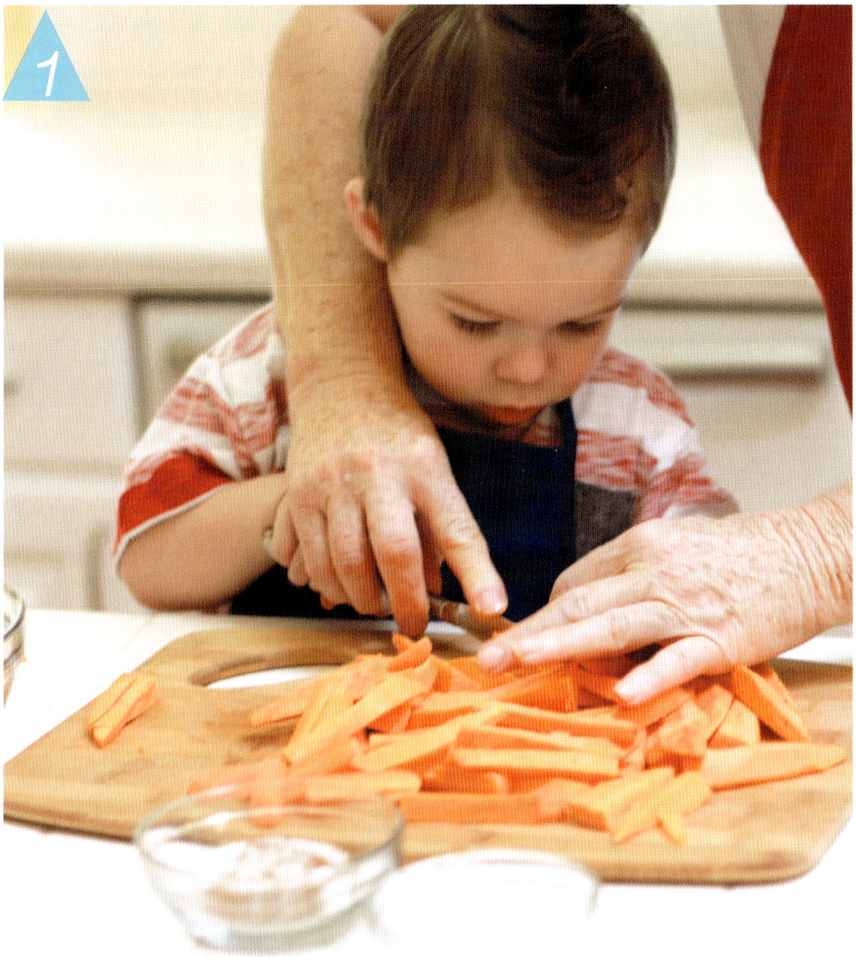
1

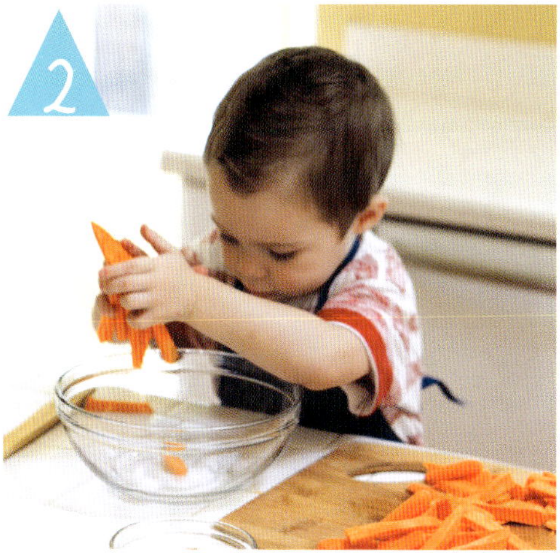
2

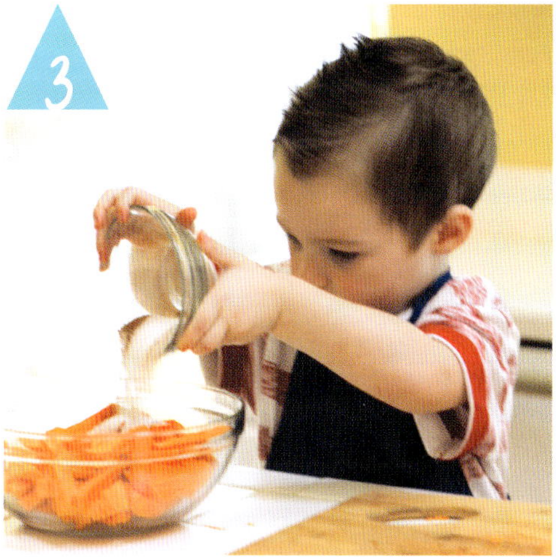
3

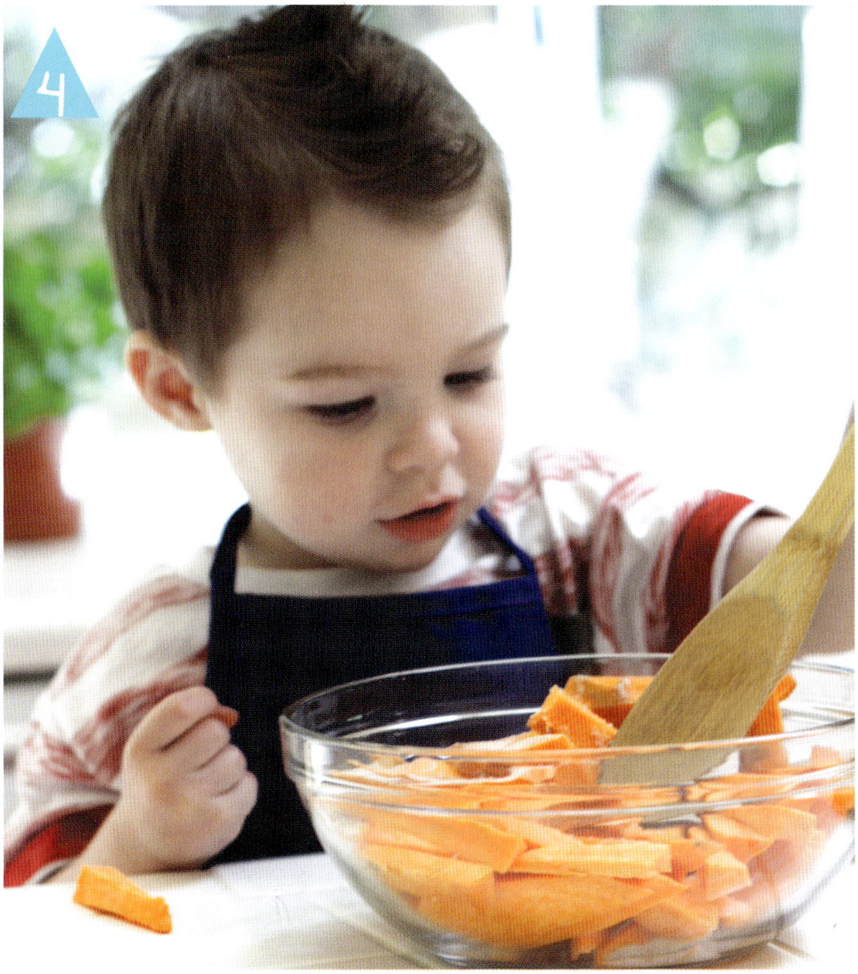
4

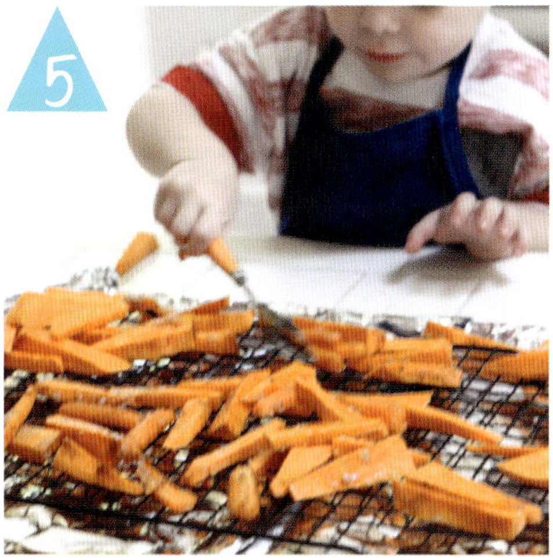
5

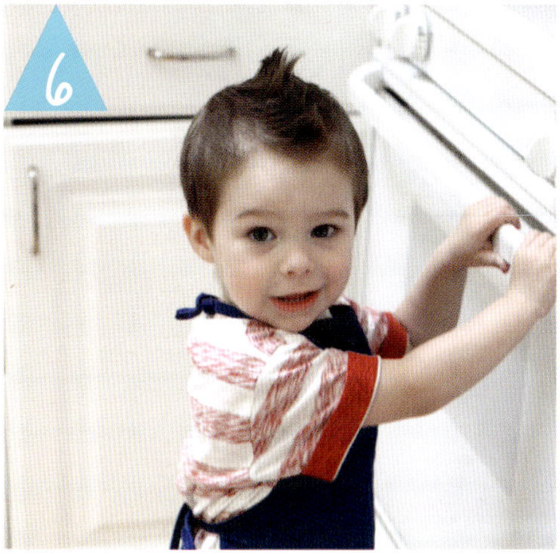
6

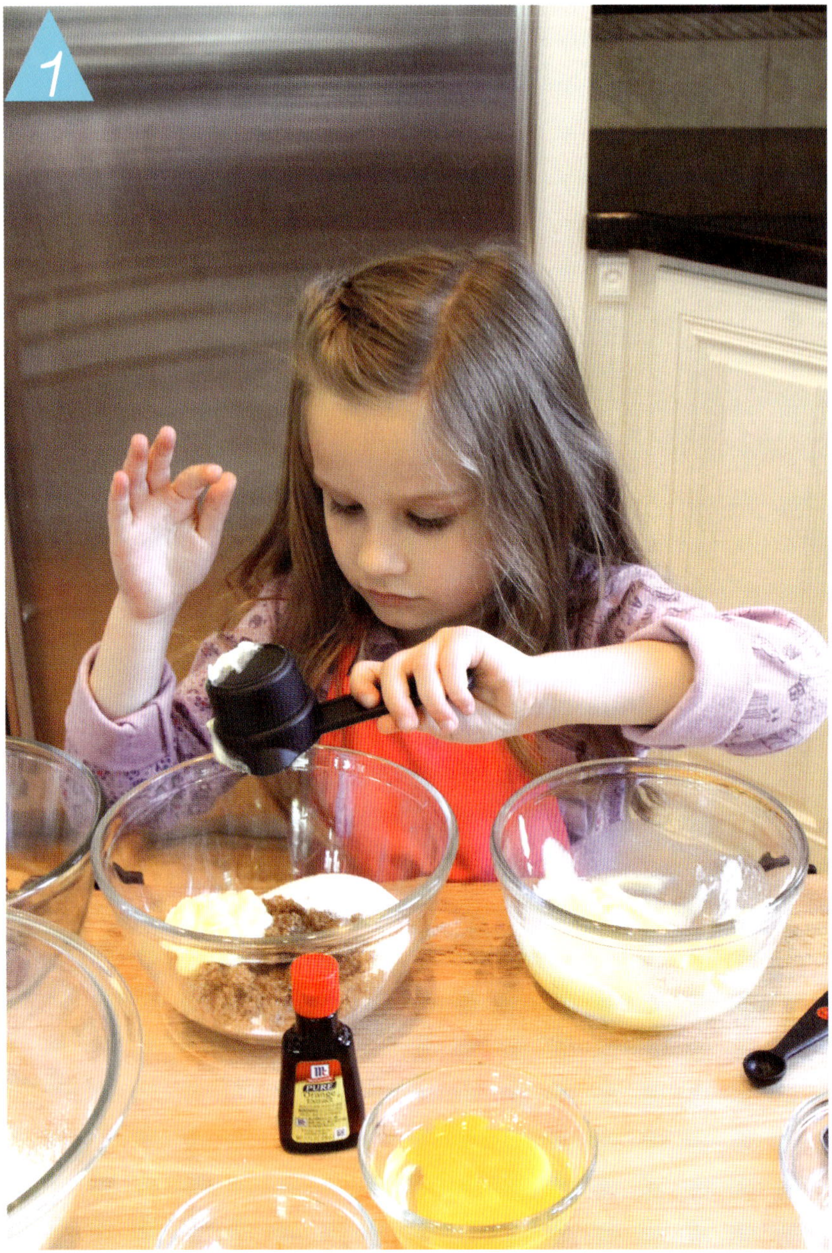
1
PURE

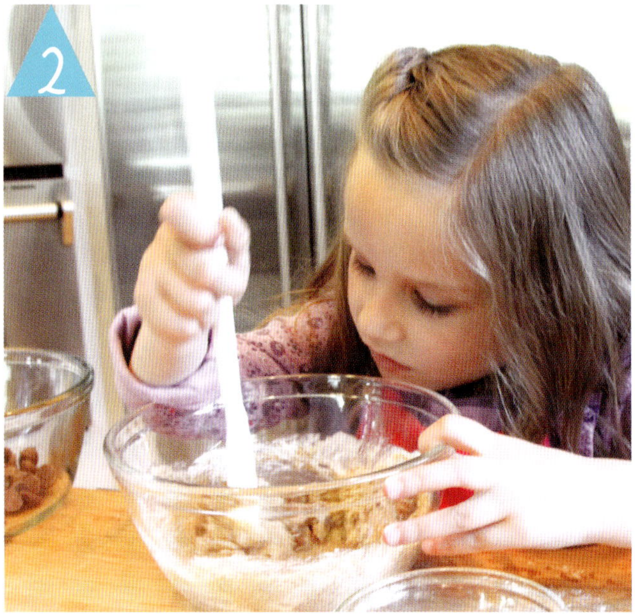
2

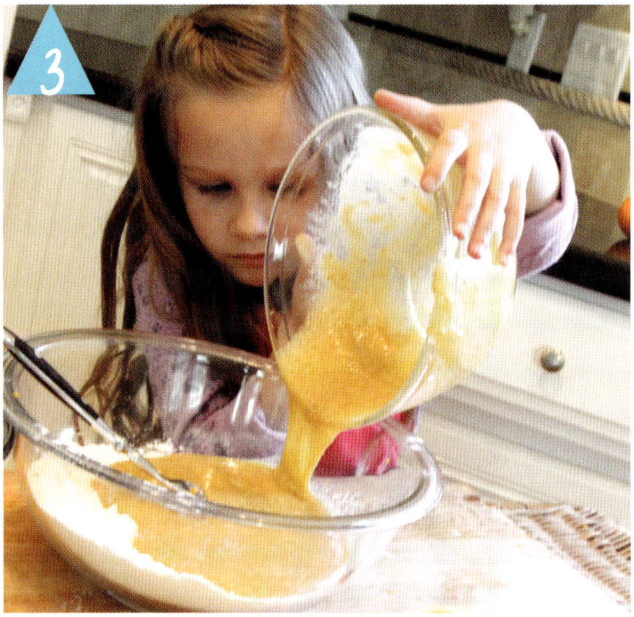
3

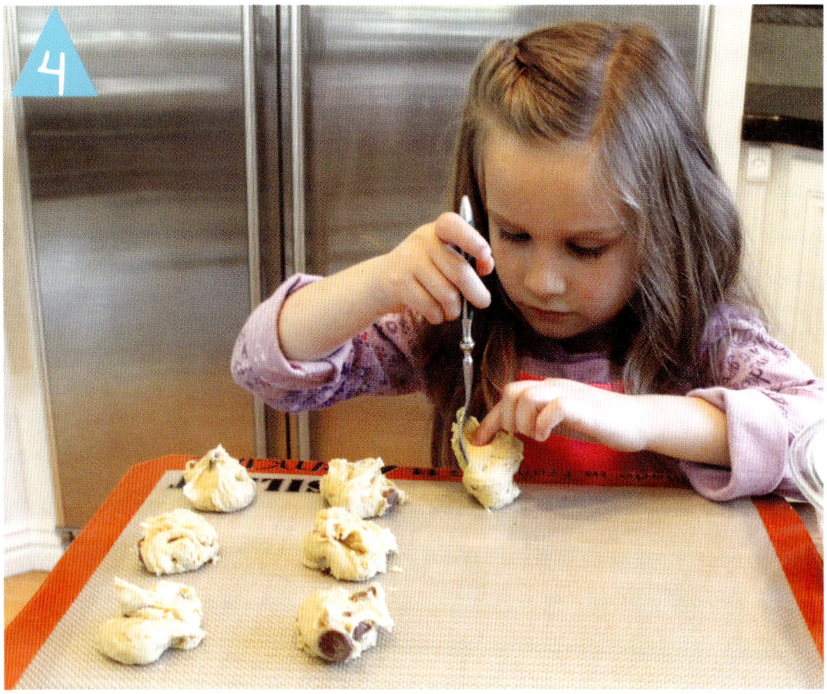
4

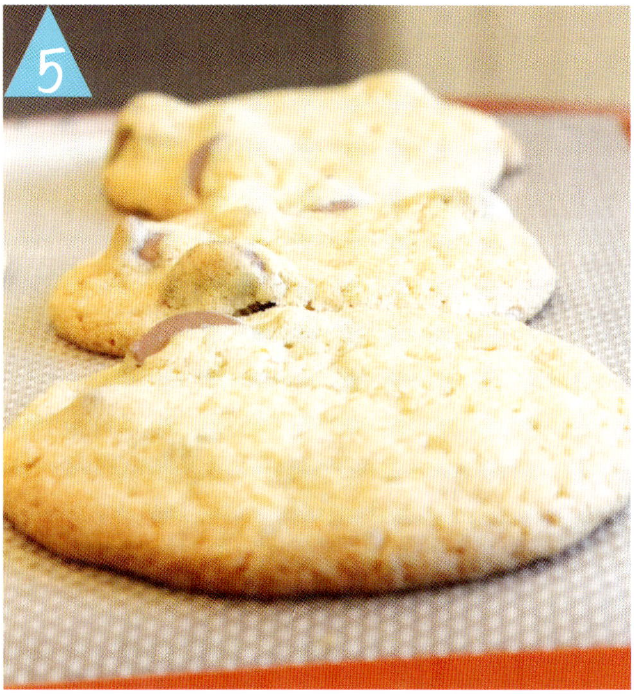
5

Orange Chocolate Chip Cookies
(serves 4)

DIRECTIONS

1. Preheat the oven to 350 degrees.
2. If the butter is hard, microwave it in a microwave-safe bowl for 10 seconds. Heat it for 5 more seconds after that until it is soft. Let the butter sit until you are ready to use it.
3. Zest the orange by running a zester over the orange peel. Do this softly until you have about 2 tablespoons of orange zest.
4. Put the white and brown sugar in a large bowl. Add the softened butter, vanilla, and eggs and stir.
5. Mix the flour, baking soda, and baking powder in a bowl. Add the orange zest and orange extract and mix again.
6. Add the wet ingredients to the bowl with the dry ingredients. Stir. Fold in the chocolate chips with a spoon.
7. Get a cookie sheet or baking pan. Spoon the cookie dough onto the pan.
8. Cook for 8–10 minutes, until the cookies are light brown.
9. Take the pan out of the oven with oven mitts. Let the cookies cool for about 2 minutes. Take them off the pan and move them onto a plate with a spatula.

WHAT COULD MAKE THIS EASIER?

Use chocolate chip cookie mix. Add the ingredients listed on the package, along with the orange zest and orange extract. Be sure to follow the oven temperature and time on the package.

Level of difficulty: **HARD**
(supervision for oven and zester, many recipe steps)

KITCHEN TOOLS

oven
3 bowls
stirring spoon
cookie pan
citrus zester

INGREDIENTS

½ cup butter, softened
½ cup sugar
½ cup brown sugar
2 medium eggs
1 tsp. baking powder
1 tsp. baking soda
1¾ cups flour
½ cup chocolate chips
2 Tbsp. orange zest
1 tsp. orange extract

FOOD GROUPS

Grain	flour
Fruit	orange
Protein	eggs

Orange o 15

KITCHEN TOOLS

2 tall drinking glasses
1 long spoon
measuring spoons

INGREDIENTS

2 cups cold carrot juice
3-4 tsp. agave to sweeten (optional)
1/8 tsp. cinnamon
1/8 tsp. vanilla
1-2 scoops vanilla ice cream

FOOD GROUPS

Vegetable	carrot
Dairy	ice cream

Bunny Hop Float
(serves 2)

DIRECTIONS

1. Pour 1 cup of carrot juice into each glass.
2. In each glass, add 2 teaspoons of agave to sweeten. If you use sugar instead of agave, use 3 teaspoons.
3. Add cinnamon and vanilla to both glasses. Stir well with a spoon.
4. Add 1 scoop of ice-cream to each glass. Put a straw and a long spoon into each glass. Eat a spoonful of ice cream with the juice, and drink it with the straw when it starts to melt.

WHAT ELSE CAN YOU DO?

For a different taste, you can make a float with plain orange juice. Add a scoop of vanilla ice cream.

Level of difficulty: **EASY**

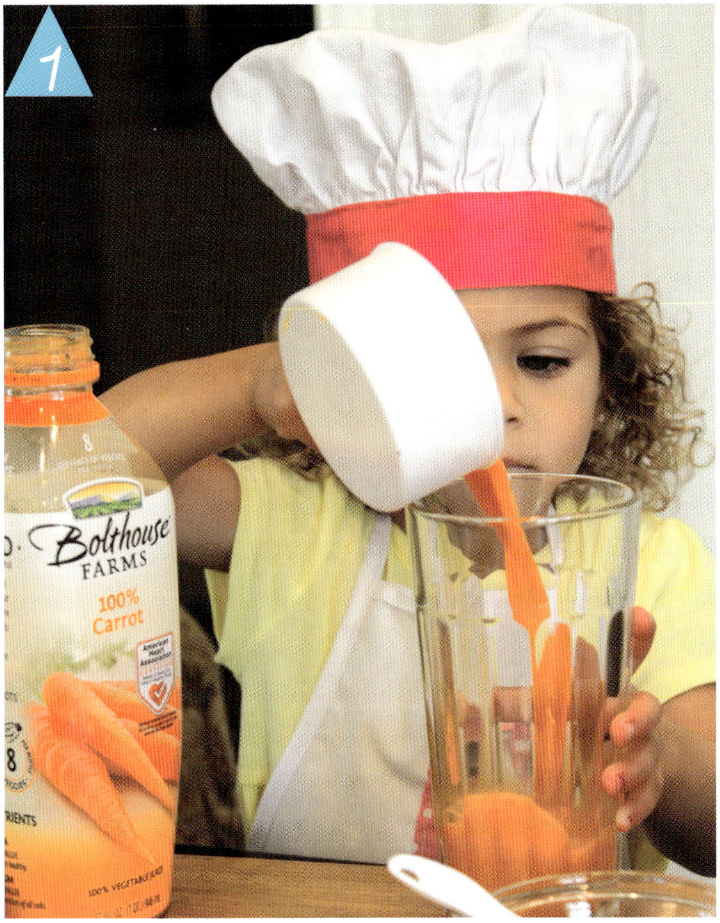
1
Bolthouse
FARMS
100%
Carrot

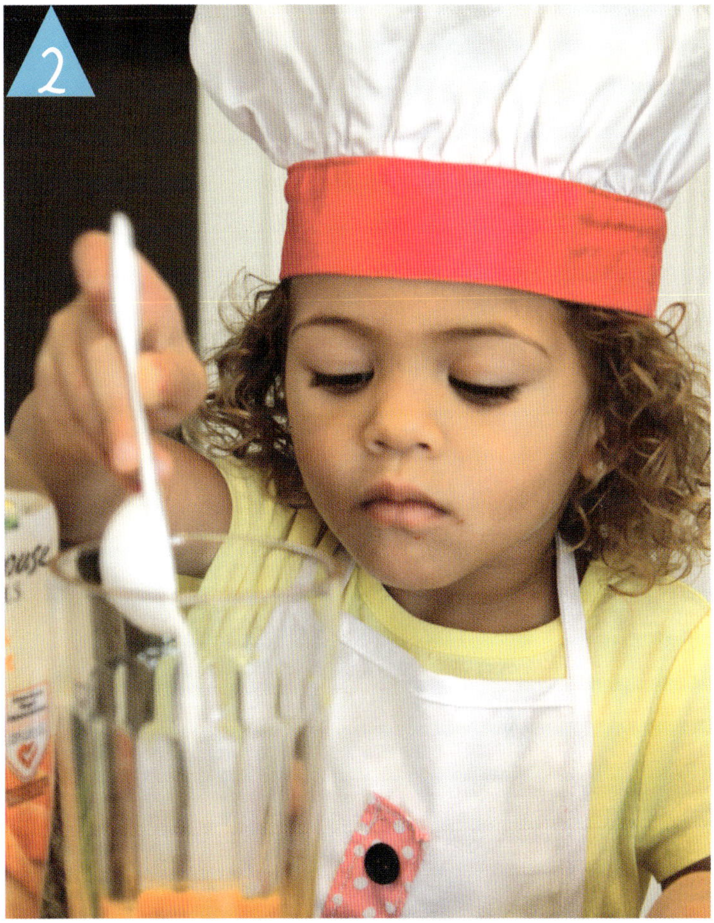
2

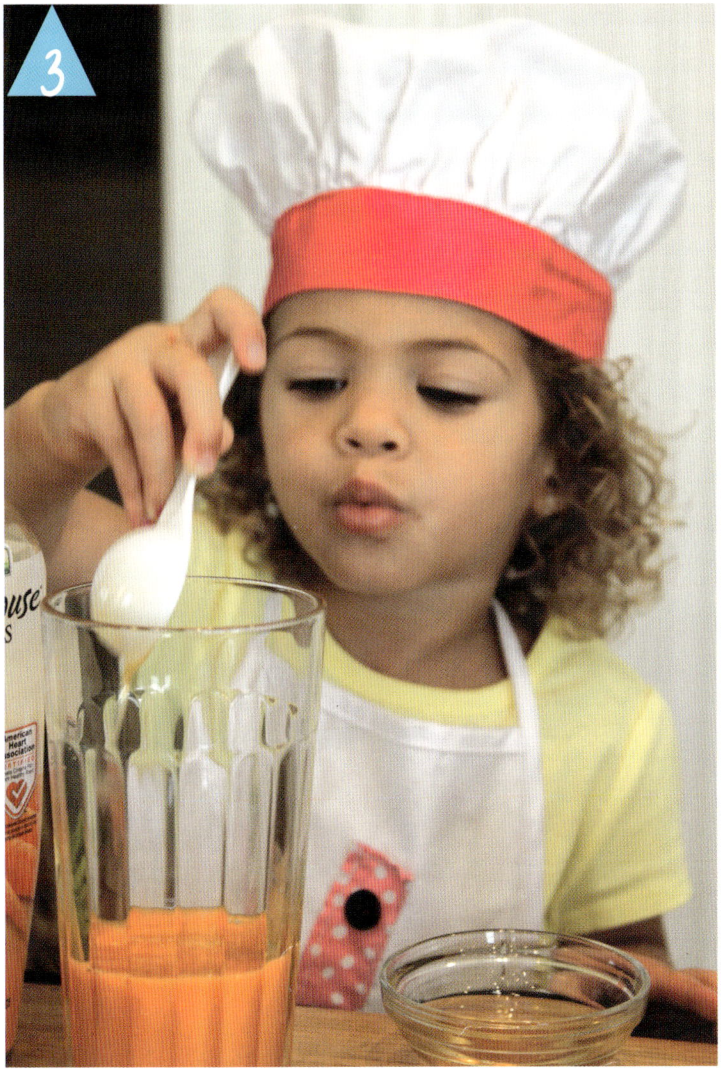
3

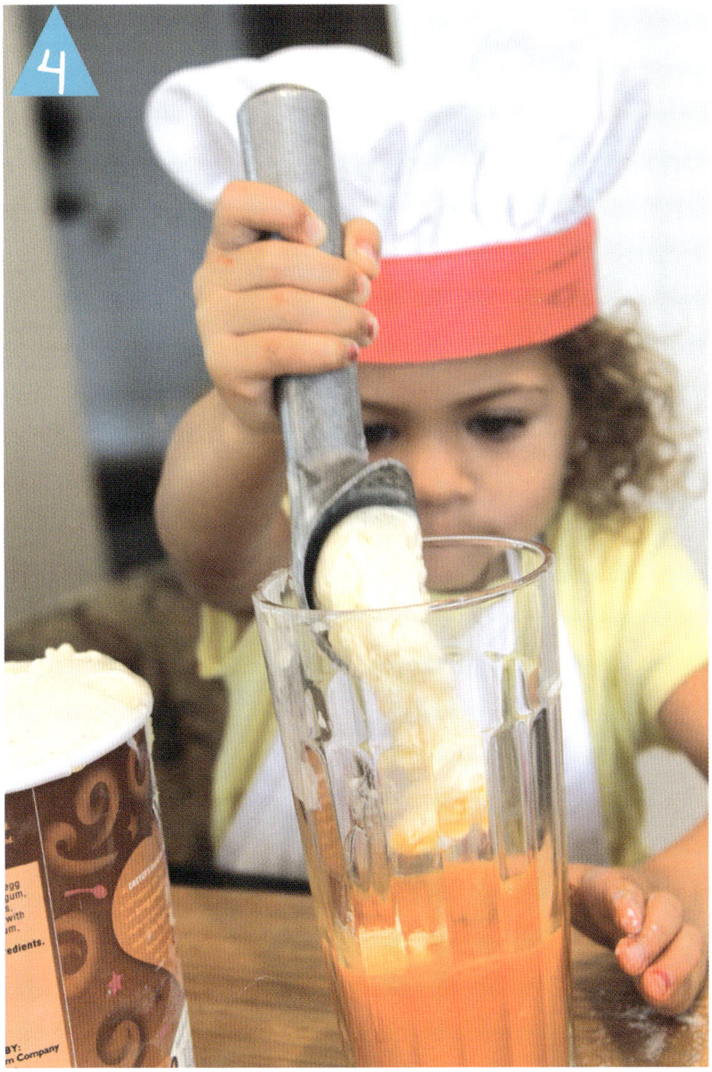
4

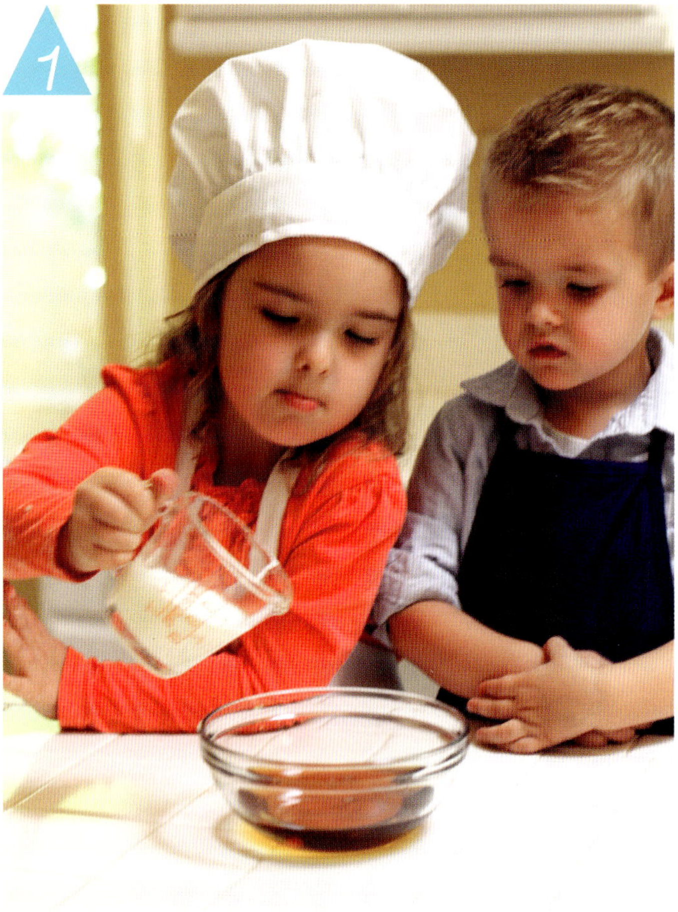
1

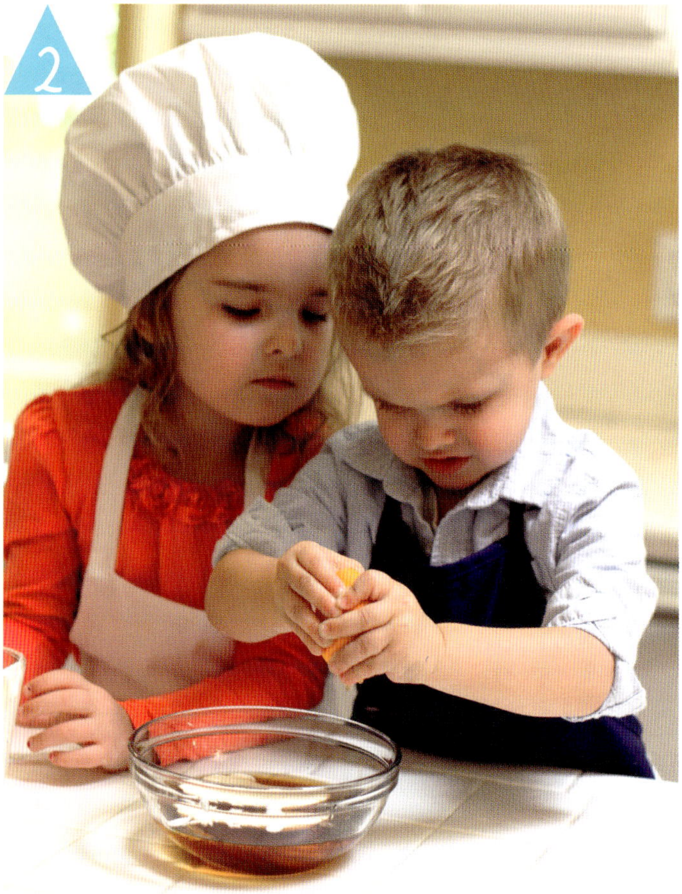
2

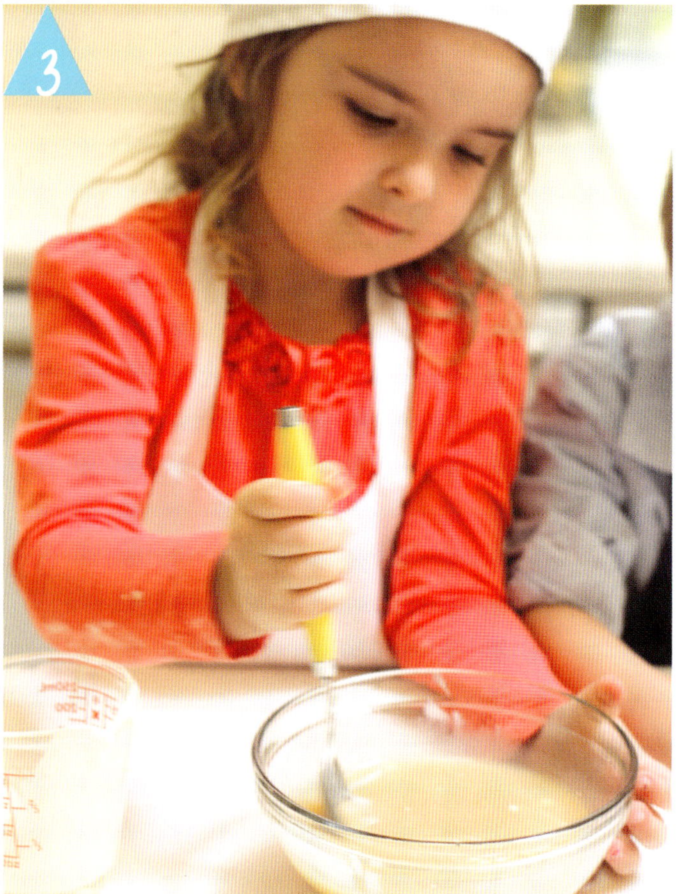
3

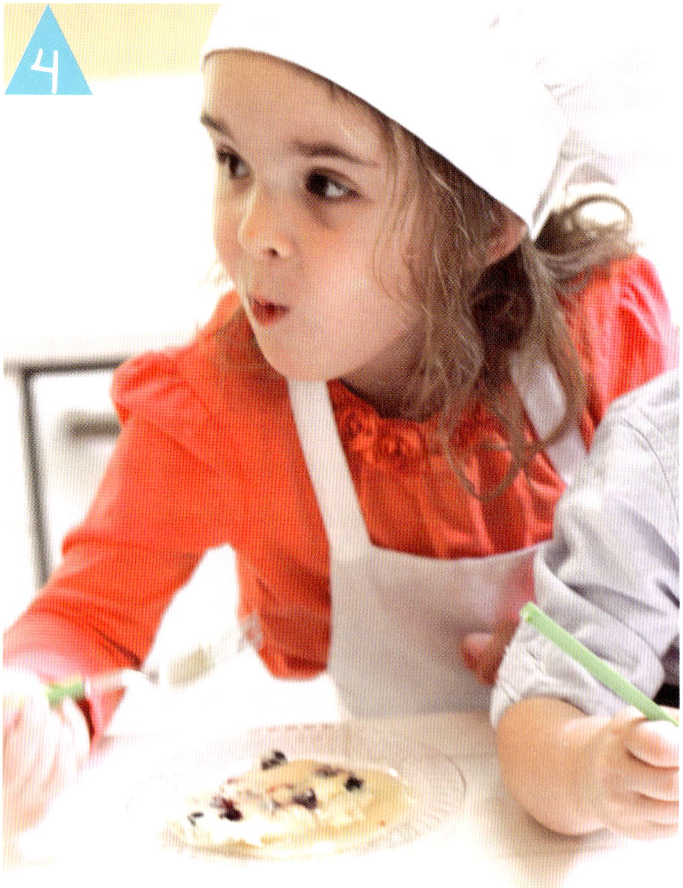
4

Creamy Orange Syrup

(serves 3)

DIRECTIONS

1. Pour the maple syrup into a bowl.
2. Add the yogurt to the bowl.
3. Cut the orange in half, and squeeze the juice from the orange into a bowl. Or, if you are using orange juice, simply pour it into the bowl.
4. Add the vanilla to the bowl.
5. Mix everything together.
6. Pour your syrup on pancakes, granola, or cupcakes.

WHAT ELSE CAN YOU DO?

Try using lemon or apple juice instead of orange juice.

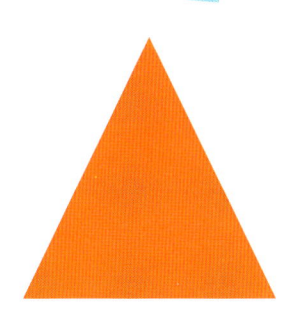

Level of difficulty: EASY
(supervision required if orange is cut for juice)

KITCHEN TOOLS

bowl
spoon
butter knife

INGREDIENTS

1 cup maple syrup
¼ cup plain yogurt
½ orange (or 2 Tbsp. orange juice)
1 tsp. vanilla

FOOD GROUPS

| Dairy | yogurt |
| Fruit | orange |

Orange • 19

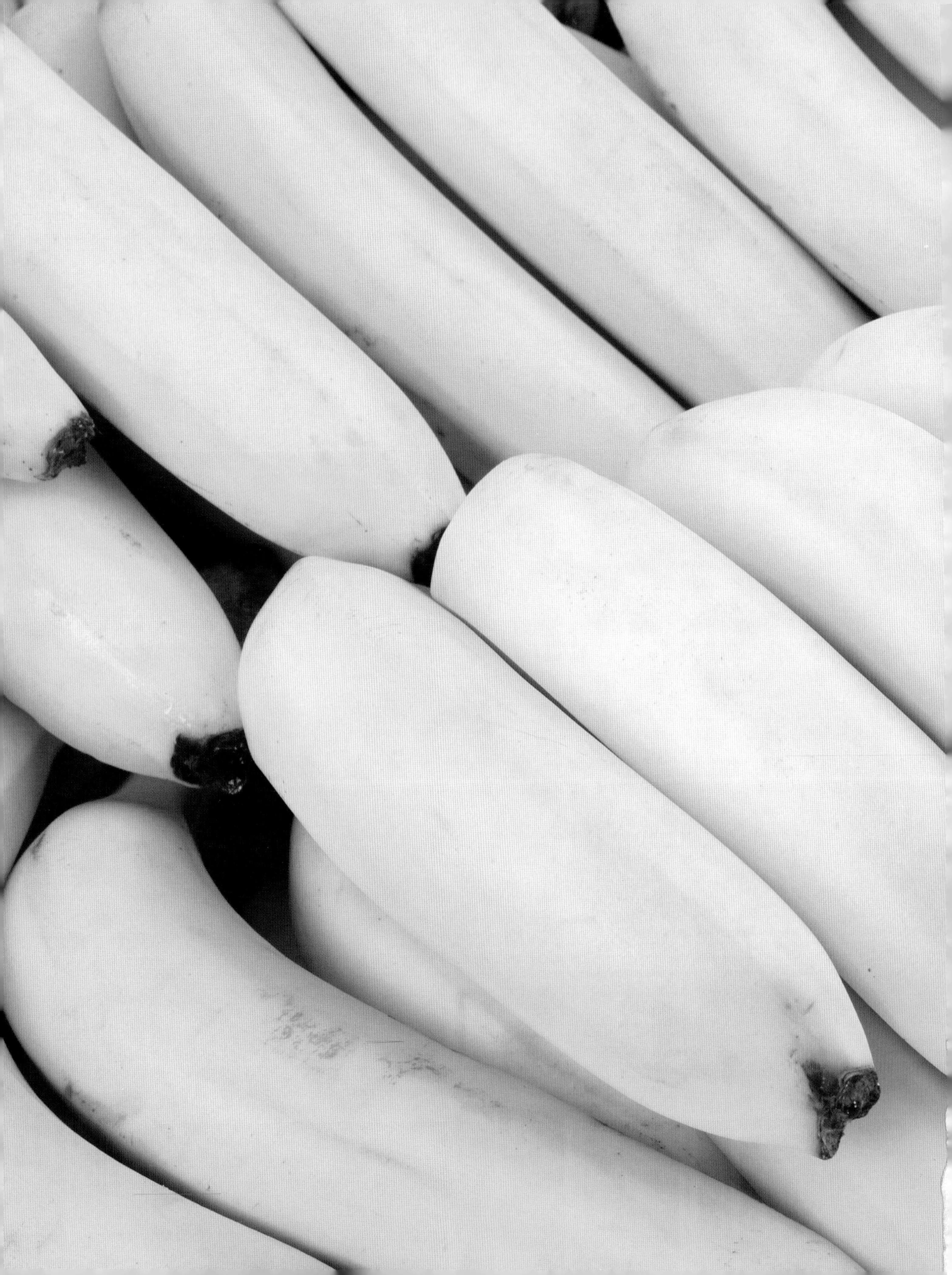

YELLOW

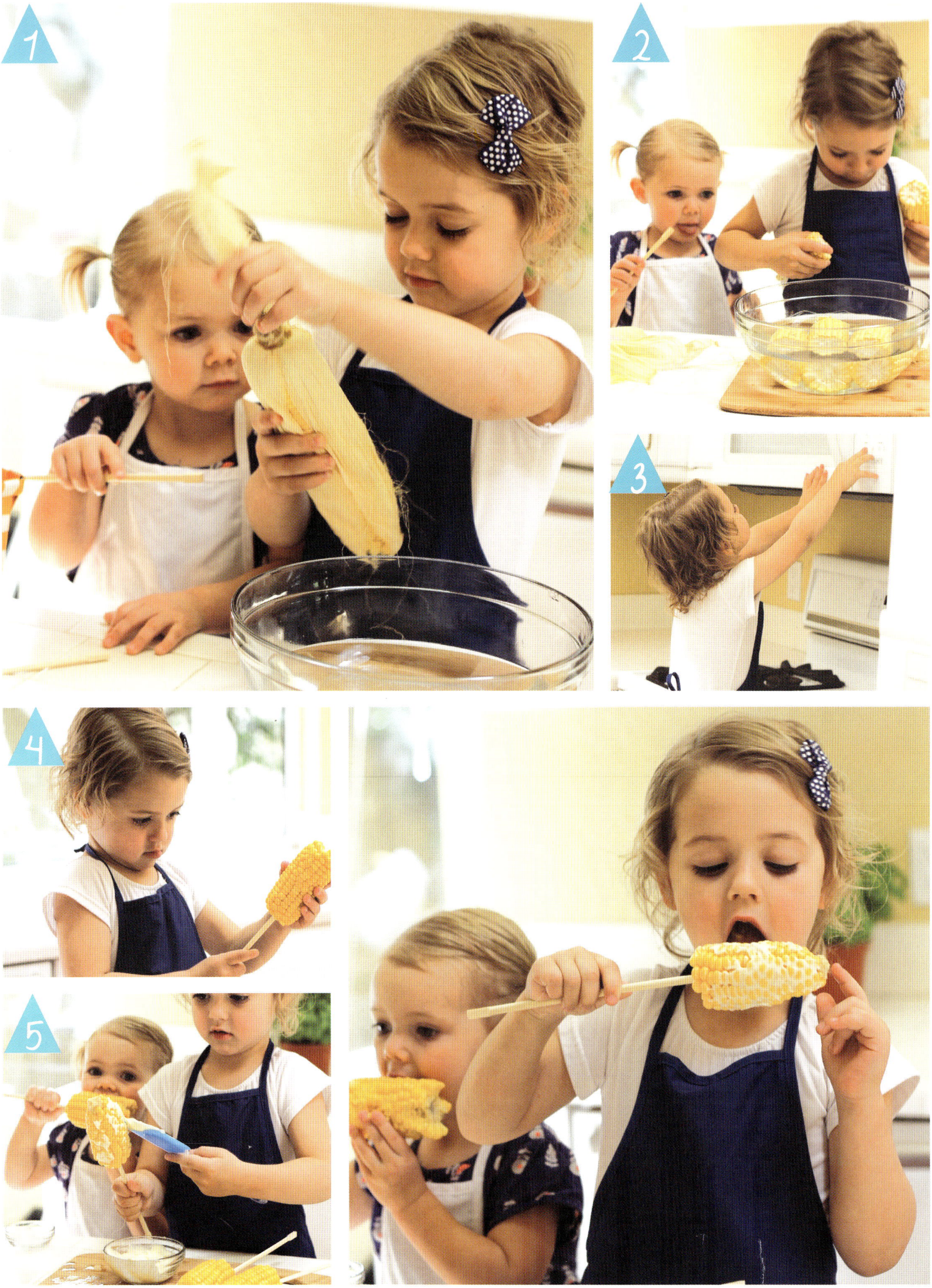
1
2
3
4
5

Ready Set Go Corn on a Stick

(serves 3)

DIRECTIONS

1. Shuck the corn by taking off the leaves and the silk.
2. Break the corn in half—ask an adult for help if you need to.
3. Put the halves of corn in a bowl. Add water until it is about two fingers' width from the top of the bowl.
4. Put the bowl in the microwave and cook for 4 minutes.
5. With the help of an adult, check the corn to see if it is done. Put a fork in the corn to see if it is soft enough to eat. If it isn't done, cook it for 4 more minutes and check it again.
6. With an adult, take the corn out of the microwave with hot pads. Let a grown-up carefully take the hot corn out of the bowl.
7. Let the corn cool for about 10 minutes. Put the end of the corn on a skewer. Put butter on the corn with a butter knife, or spread a mayonnaise/salt mixture onto the corn.

WHAT ELSE YOU CAN DO?

Add a small amount of cayenne pepper for color. Start out with just a little bit so it isn't too hot.

You can also try using ranch dressing instead of butter.

Instead of using butter, mix three tablespoons of mayonnaise with ¼ teaspoon of garlic salt and spread this on your corn.

Level of difficulty: HARD
(adult to take corn out of microwave and bowl when hot)

KITCHEN TOOLS

large microwave-safe bowl
microwave
hot pads
wooden or metal skewers

INGREDIENTS

3 ears of corn
3 Tbsp. butter, softened

FOOD GROUPS

Vegetable | corn

Yellow o 23

KITCHEN TOOLS

blender
knife
cutting board
freezer-proof container
bowl
ice cream scoop

INGREDIENTS

1 can strained pineapple
3 Tbsp. orange juice
½ cup almond milk
⅓ sugar or agave

FOOD GROUPS

Fruit	pineapple
Grain	almond milk
Dairy	milk (if you use milk instead of almond milk)

24 o Wick

Frozen Pineapple Fluff
(serves 3)

DIRECTIONS

1. Open the can of pineapple by pulling the tab or by using a can opener.
2. Strain the juice from the can. Pour the pineapple into a blender.
3. Add the almond milk and the cane sugar or agave. Let it blend on high for 3 minutes. Taste it with a spoon to see if it's sweet enough.
4. Pour the mixture into a plastic container and freeze it for at least 3 hours.
5. It should be frozen enough to eat. Use an ice cream scoop to scoop the mixture into a bowl. Fluff it up with a fork.
6. Enjoy!

WHAT YOU CAN DO DIFFERENTLY?

Try having an adult cut a fresh pineapple. Use 1 cup of fresh pineapple instead of using canned pineapple.

Level of difficulty: **MEDIUM**
(use of can opener and blender)

1
2
3
4

Banana Split Cups

(serves 5)

KITCHEN TOOLS

knife
cutting board
plastic cups

INGREDIENTS

5 hard coconut cookies
2 bananas
10 strawberries
vanilla ice cream
1 small jar chocolate sauce
1 small jar maraschino cherries
whipped cream

FOOD GROUPS

Grain	cookie
Fruit	strawberries
	bananas
	cherry
Dairy	ice cream
	whipped cream

DIRECTIONS

1. Break the coconut cookies into small pieces with your hands.
2. Remove the skin from the banana. Cut the banana into small 1-inch pieces.
3. Wash the strawberries and cut the green ends off. Cut the strawberries in small pieces.
4. Fill each cup with cookies pieces.
5. Add some banana pieces. Add the same amount of strawberry pieces.
6. Add 1 scoop of ice cream on top of the fruit.
7. Pour chocolate sauce on top of the ice cream.
8. Add whipped cream and a cherry on top.

WHAT ELSE CAN YOU DO?

Try using frozen yogurt instead of ice cream.

26 o Wick

Level of difficulty: **EASY**
(adult supervision for cutting fruit)

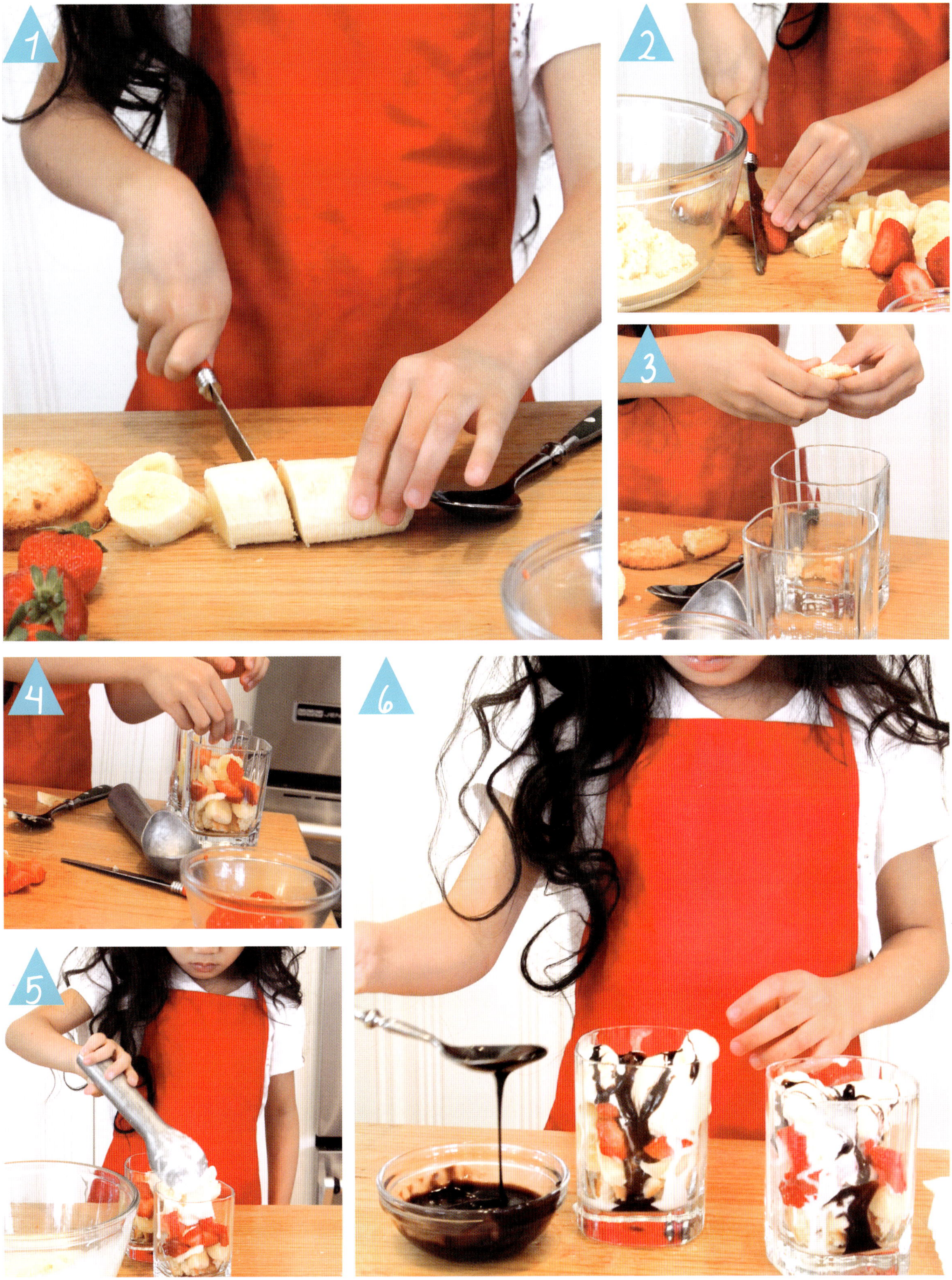
1
2
3
4
5
6

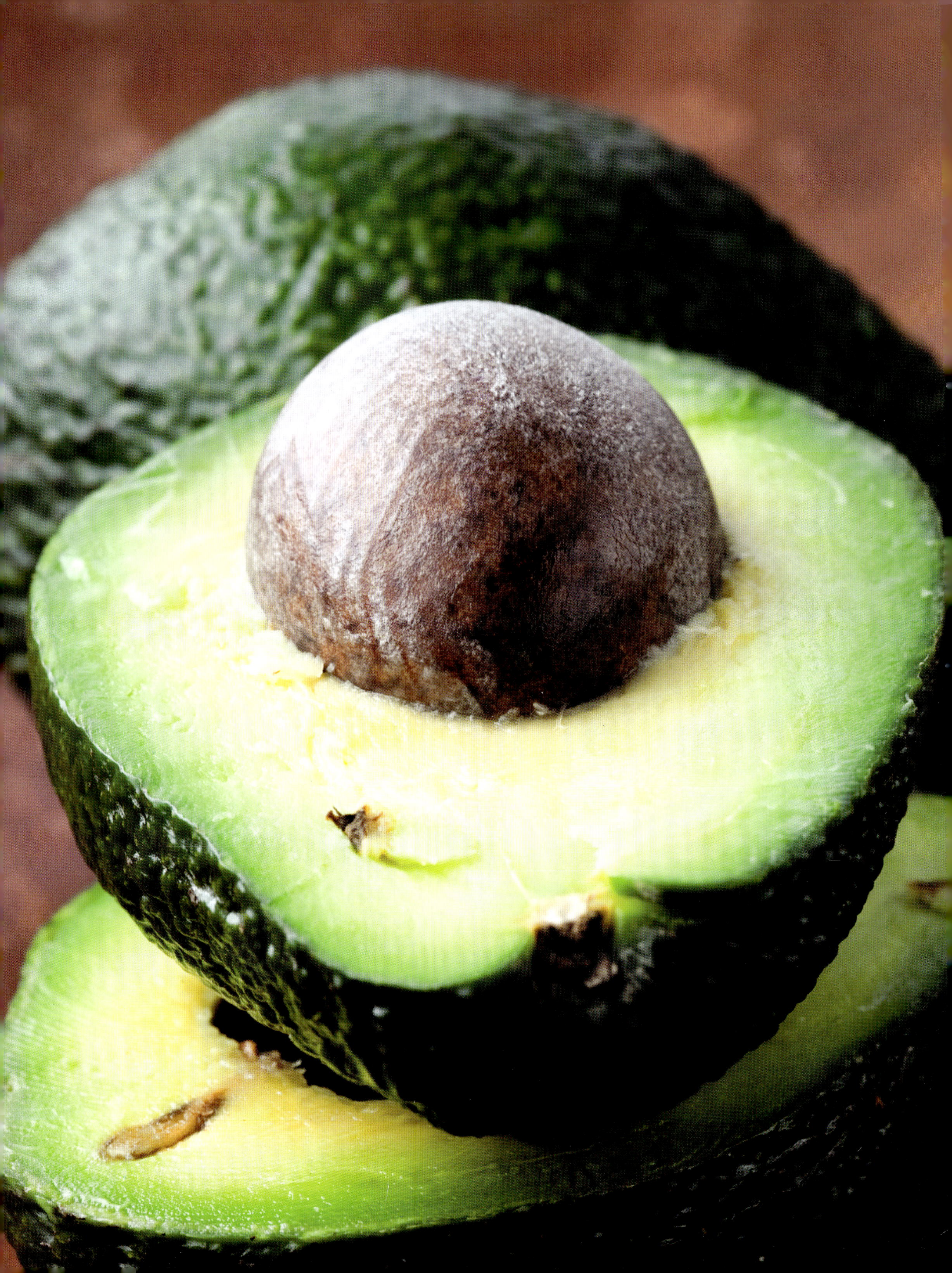

GREEN

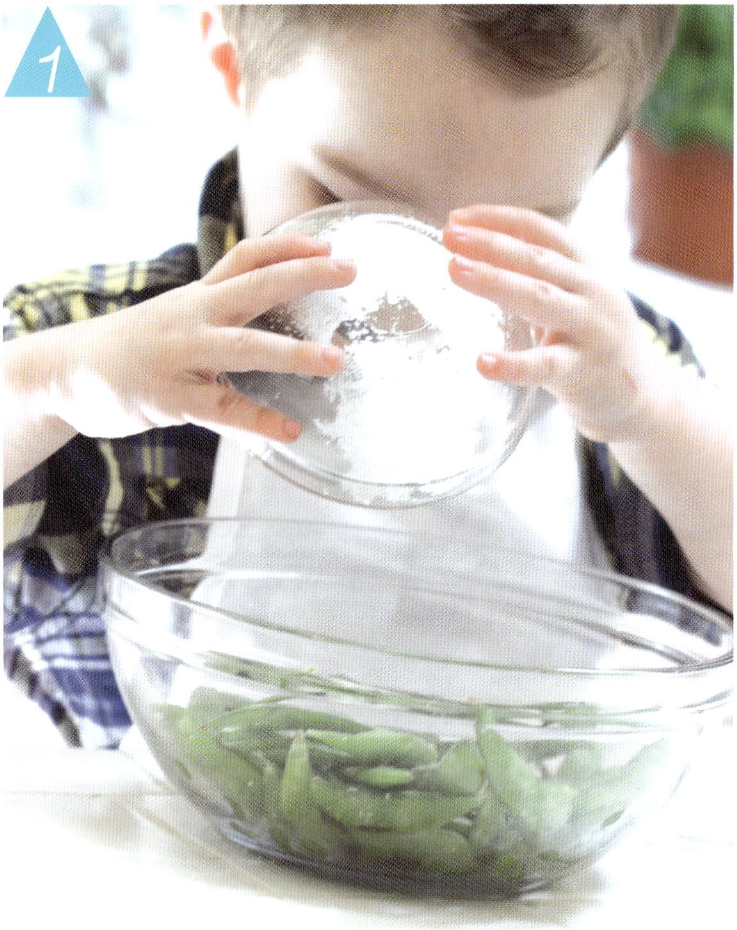
1
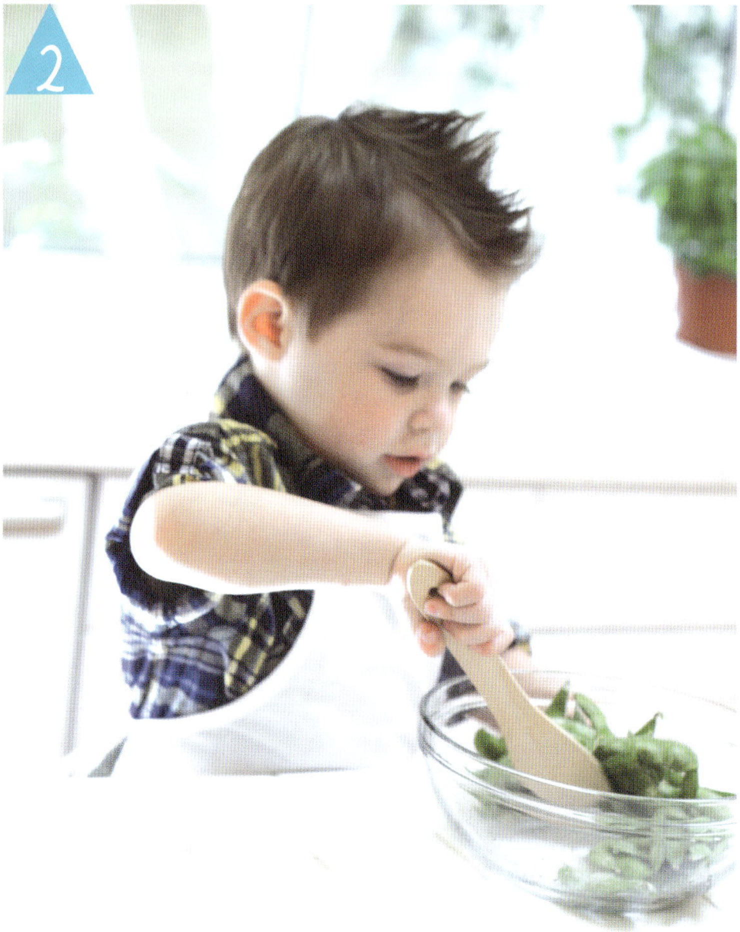
2
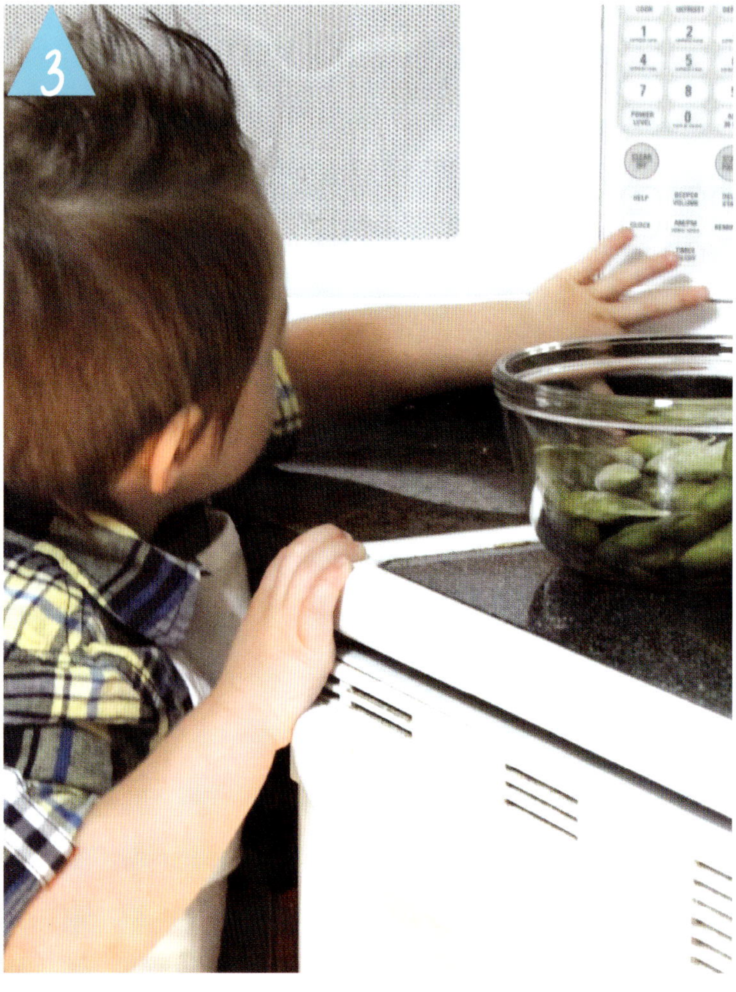
3
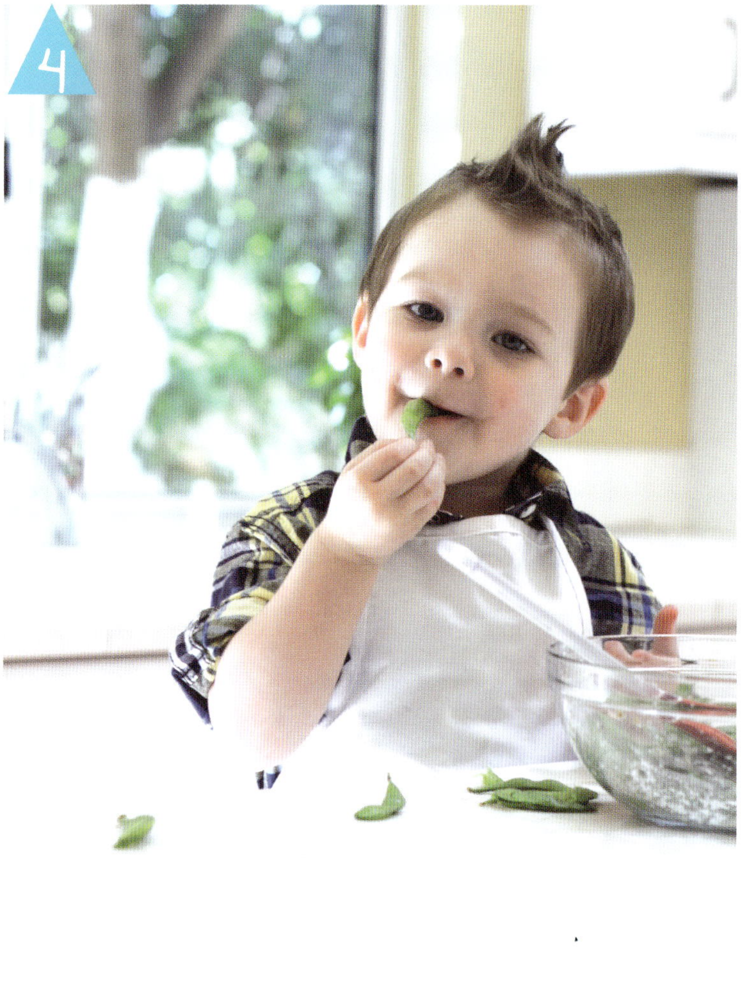
4

Zesty Edamame
(serves 6)

DIRECTIONS

1. Put the frozen edamame in a medium bowl. Add 1 teaspoon of water to the bowl.
2. Add a few drops of olive oil to the bowl. Then add the lemon or orange zest and the sea salt.
3. Stir well.
4. Put the bowl in the microwave for the length of time instructed on the package. Let the edamame cool when they are done cooking.
5. Eat the edamame by holding onto one end as you put most of the edamame pod in your mouth. Squeeze the pod with your teeth as you pull it out of your mouth. The soybeans inside the pod will pop into your mouth.

HOW CAN YOU MAKE THIS EASIER?

Try putting lemon salt on the edamame instead of lemon or orange zest.

HOW ELSE CAN YOU EAT EDAMAME?

Push the soybeans out of the pod into a bowl with your hands.

Level of difficulty EASY
(adult supervision for microwave)

KITCHEN TOOLS

microwave
medium microwave-safe bowl
teaspoon
citrus zester

INGREDIENTS

frozen edamame
sea salt
lemon or orange zest

FOOD GROUPS

| Vegetable | edamame |
| Protein | edamame |

Green • 31

Frosty Zucchini Cupcakes
(serves 12)

cheese grater
large bowl
cupcake liners
cupcake pan

INGREDIENTS

zucchini
spice cake mix
2 eggs
vegetable oil
water
your favorite frosting
candy or dried fruit (optional)

FOOD GROUPS

Grain	flour
Vegetables	zucchini
Protein	eggs

DIRECTIONS

1. Preheat the oven according to spice cake mix box instructions for cupcakes. With a cheese grater, take a clean zucchini and shred it by sliding it down the side. Shred about ¼ cup of zucchini and set it aside.

2. Pour the spice cake mix into a large bowl. Add the water, eggs, and oil. Again, follow the cake box instructions for mixing.

3. Add the zucchini and stir.

4. Put the cupcake liners in a cupcake pan. Fill each cupcake tin only a little more than half full.

5. Put the cupcakes in the oven for the length of time listed on the spice cake mix box.

6. Take the cupcakes out of the oven with oven mitts. Let a grown-up or older sibling help.

7. After the cupcakes have cooled, frost the tops of your zucchini cupcakes. Add candy or dried fruit to the top if you'd like!

WHY PUT ZUCCHINI IN CUPCAKES?

Zucchini is a popular ingredient in cupcakes and other baking because it keeps the cake moist. Zucchini cake is similar to carrot cake.

WHAT ELSE CAN YOU DO?

The grocery store has gluten-free cupcake mixes. Just add cloves and cinnamon to give it a spice flavor. Add the zucchini and cook the cupcakes as directed on the package.

Level of difficulty: **HARD**
(adult supervision for oven and zester)

32 o Wick

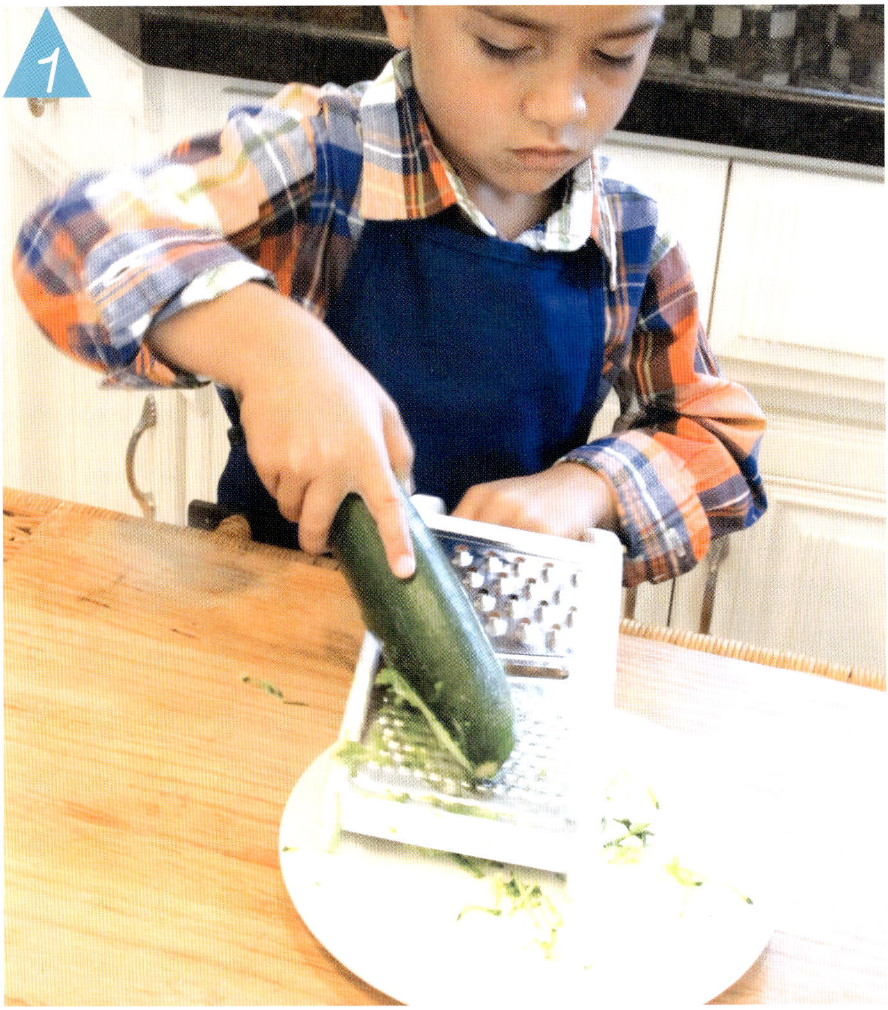
1

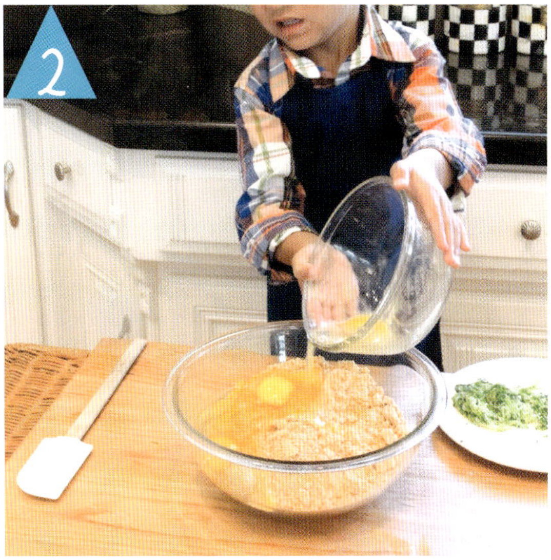
2

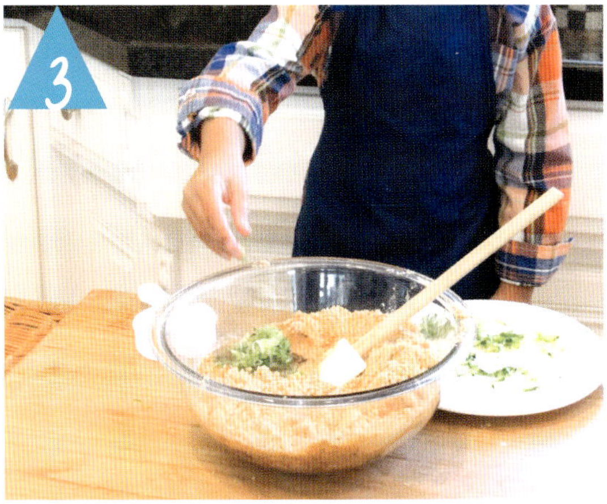
3

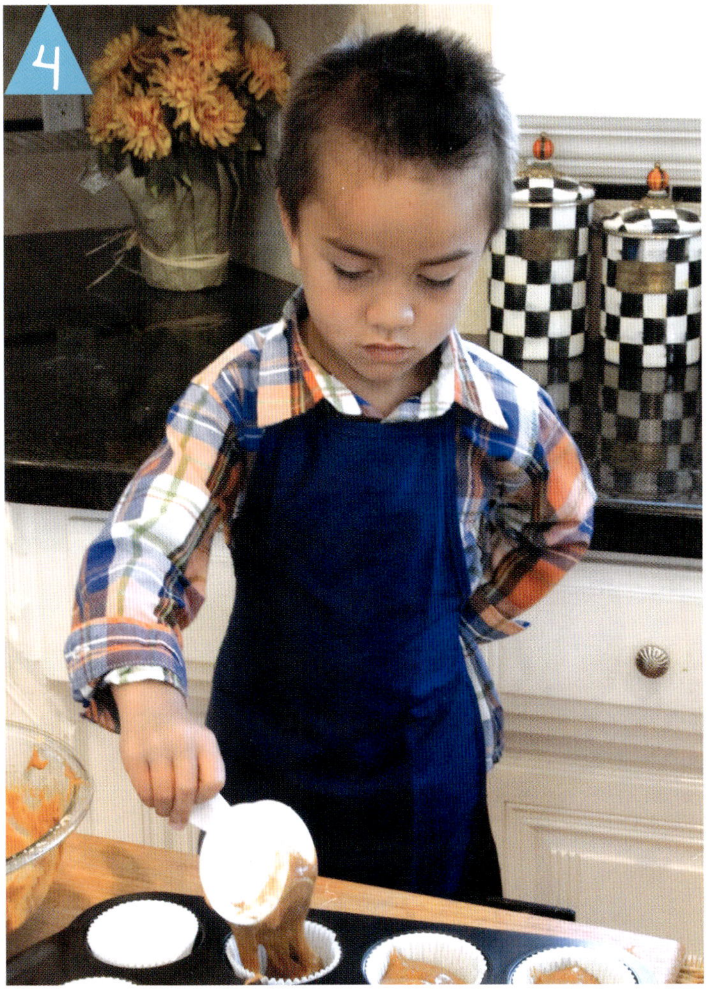
4

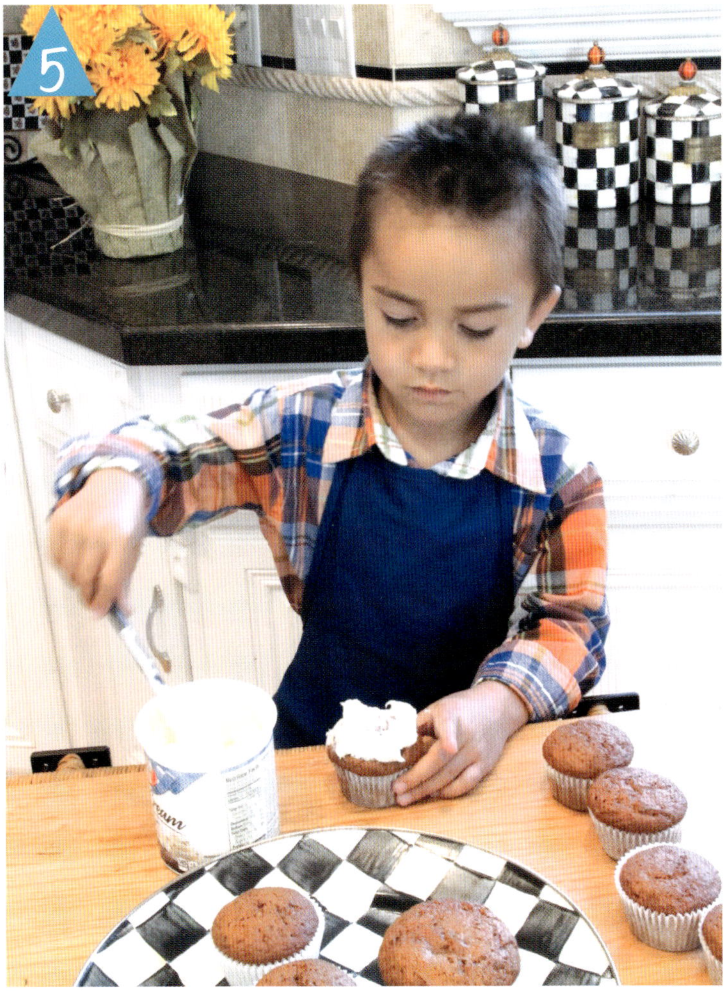
5

KITCHEN TOOLS

toaster
knife
cutting board

INGREDIENTS

1 ripe avocado (it's ripe when it's becoming soft as you press on it)
¼ tsp. salt
1 lemon or lime
2 thin bagel halves

FOOD GROUP

| Fruit/Vegetable | avocado |
| Fruit | lemon |

34 o Wick

Awesome Avocado Spread
(serves 2)

DIRECTIONS

1. Put the bagel halves in the toaster and wait until they pop up. Put them on a plate until you are ready to use them.
2. Cut out the avocado with the help of an adult. Remove the seed in the center.
3. Smash the avocado. Add salt and lime. Taste test.
4. Spread it on the bagel.

HOW DO YOU CUT AN AVOCADO?

An avocado has a very large seed. You can cut the tip of the avocado off and remove the green insides. Cut the avocado in half. Pull the avocado skin back to expose the green inside. Scoop with a spoon. This is not the only way to cut an avocado, but it's the easiest for a beginner.

WHAT ELSE CAN I DO?

Try a new taste by mixing the avocado mixture with some cream cheese. If you are sharing, this will be a easy way to make more avocado spread. This avocado spread also tastes great on toast.

Level of difficulty: **EASY**
(adult supervision for cutting avocado)

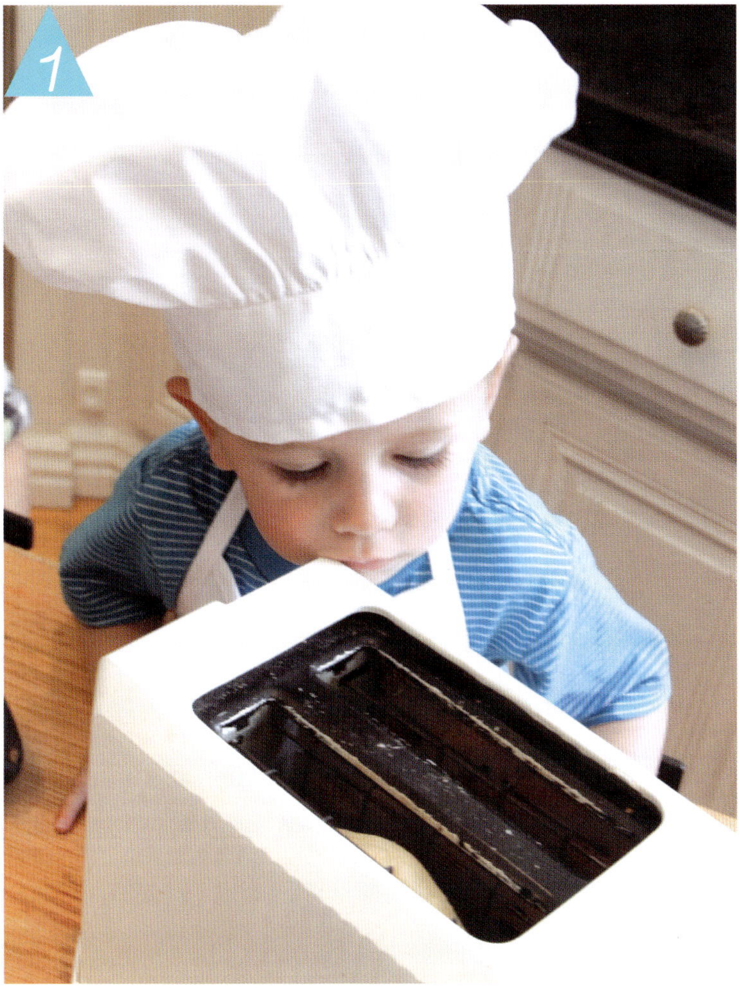
1

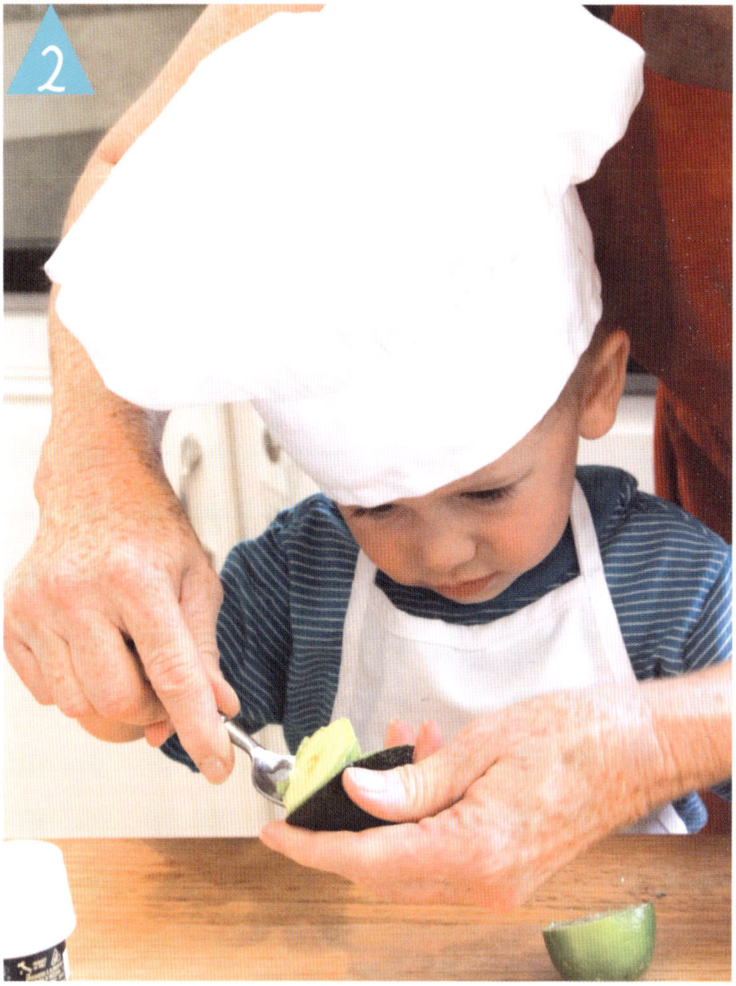
2

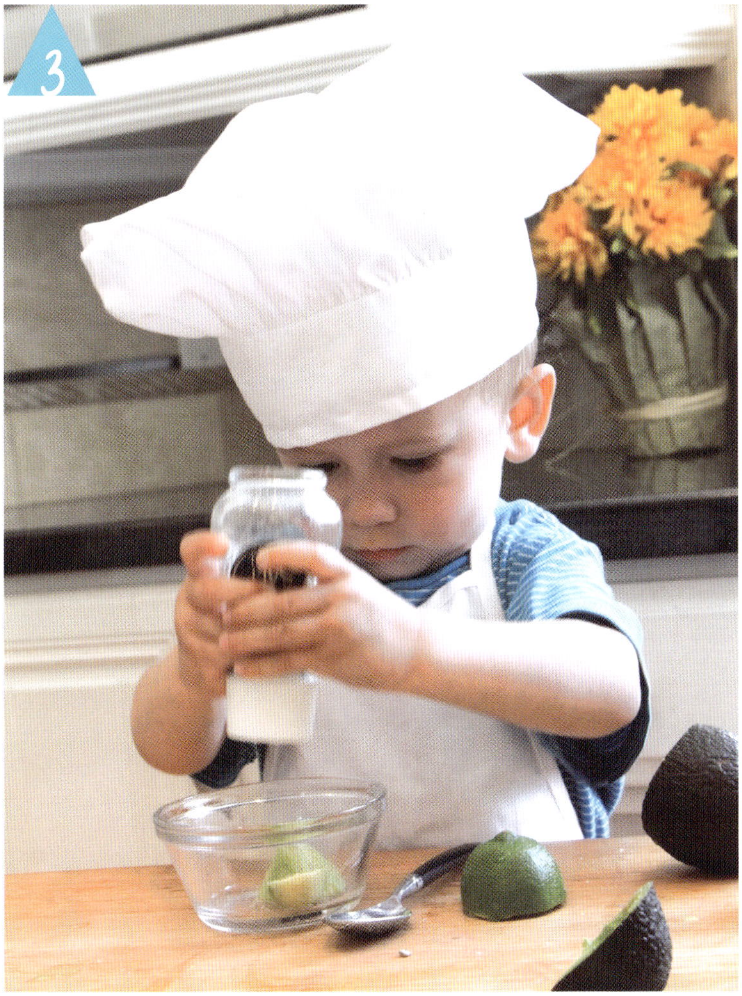
3

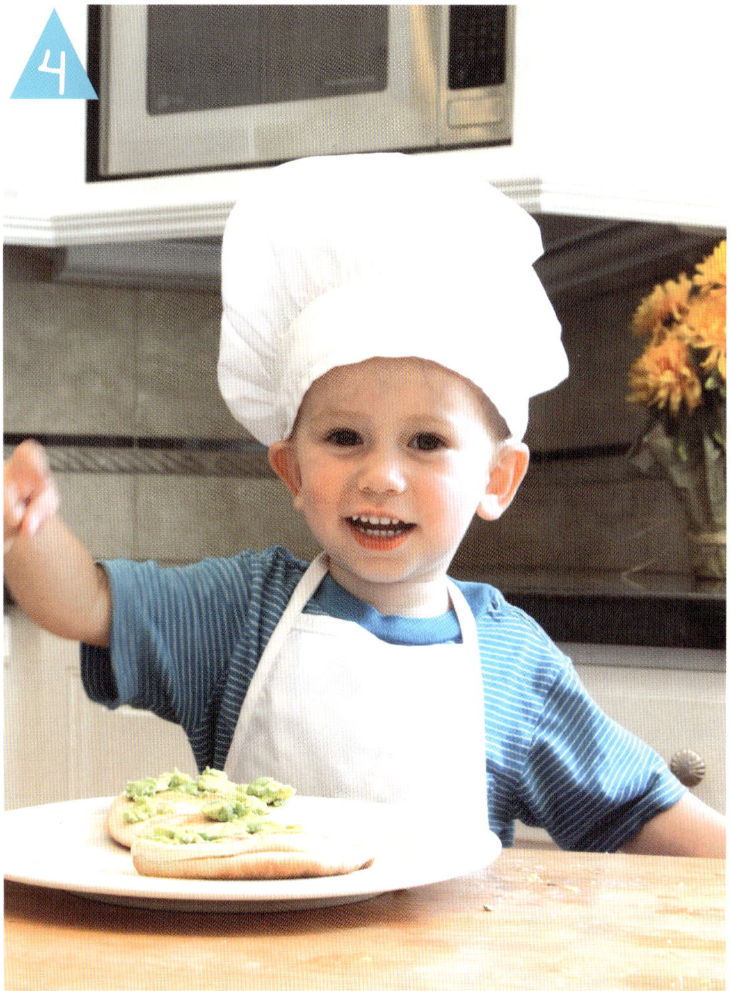
4

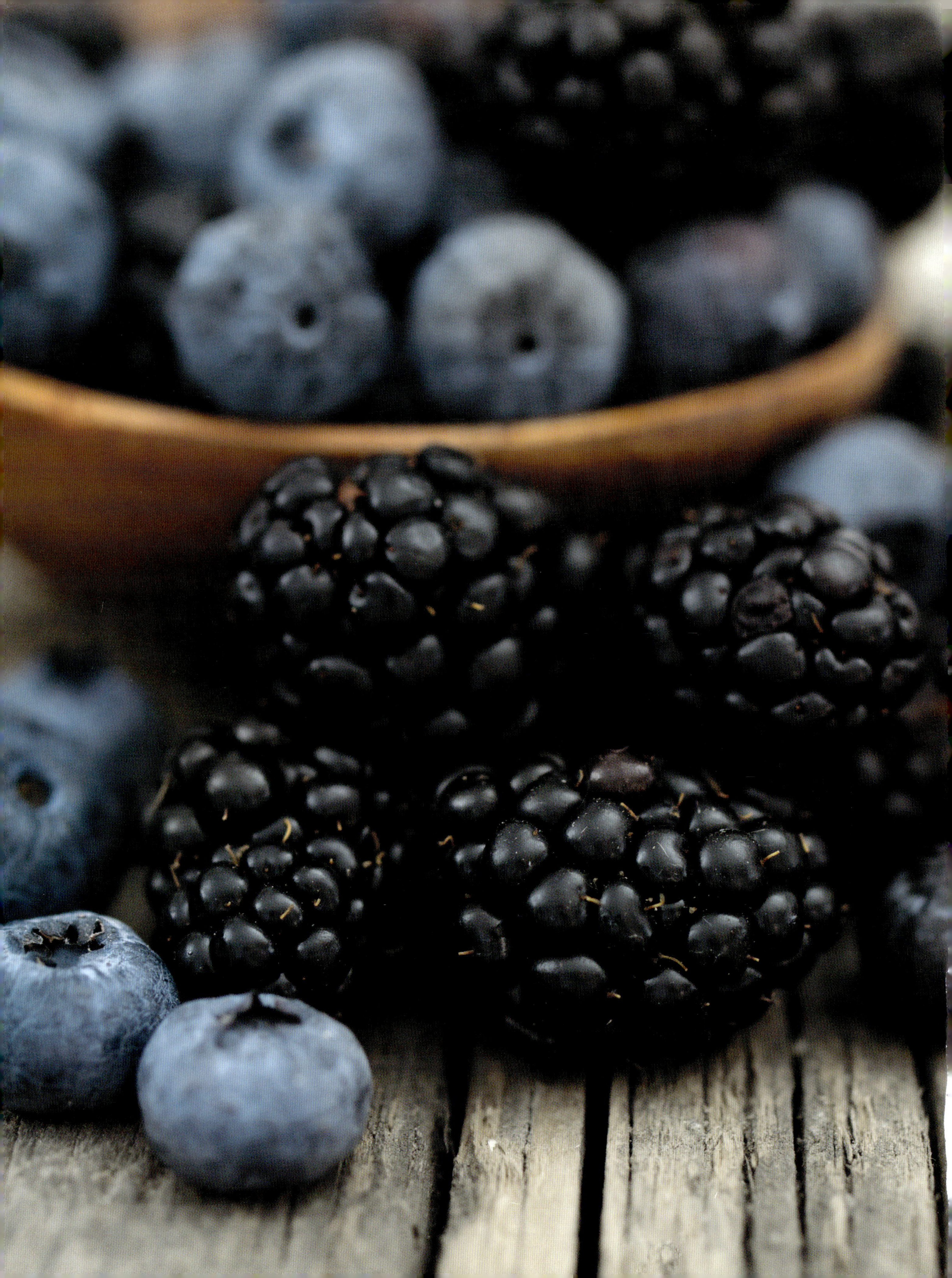

BLUE AND PURPLE

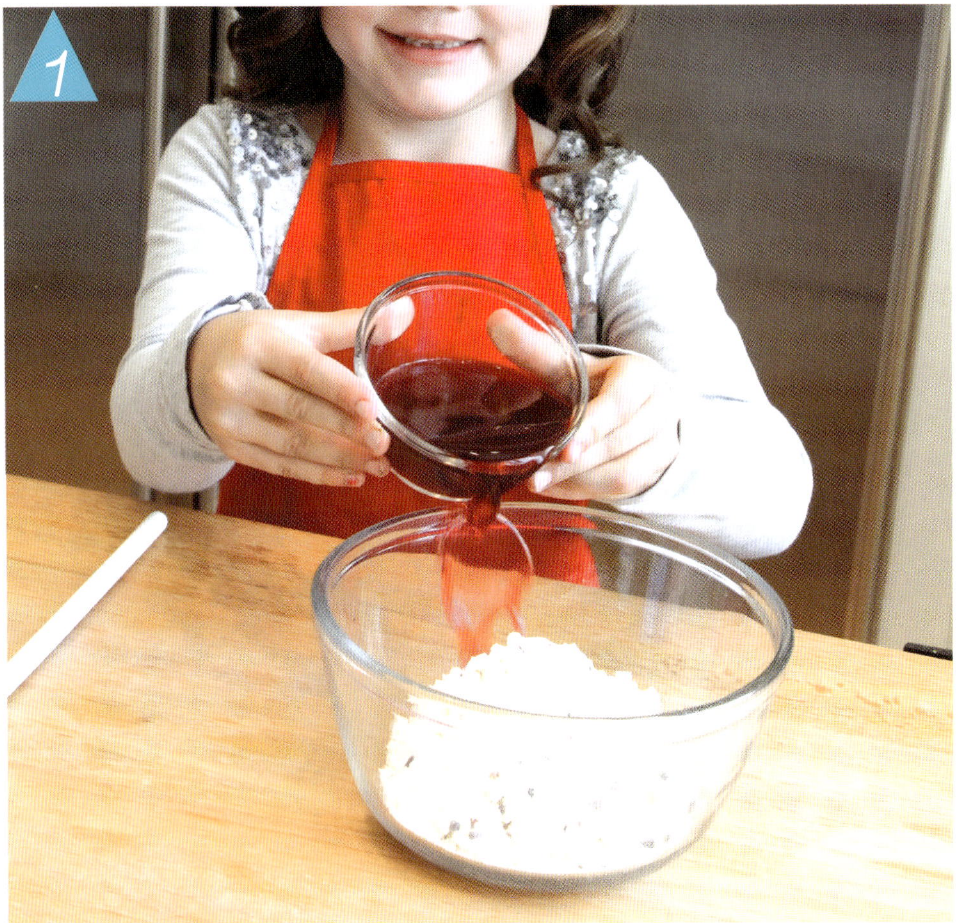
1

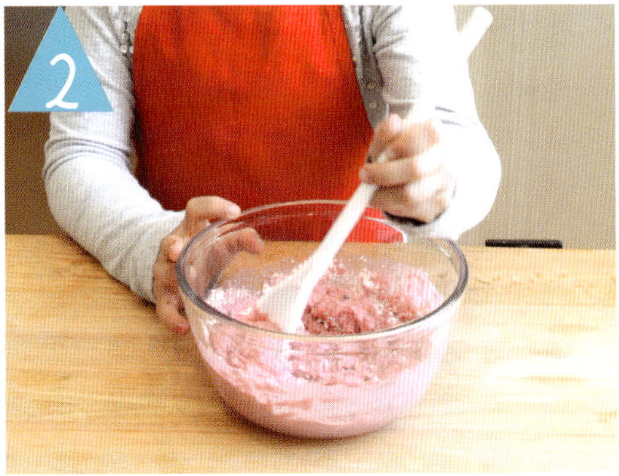
2

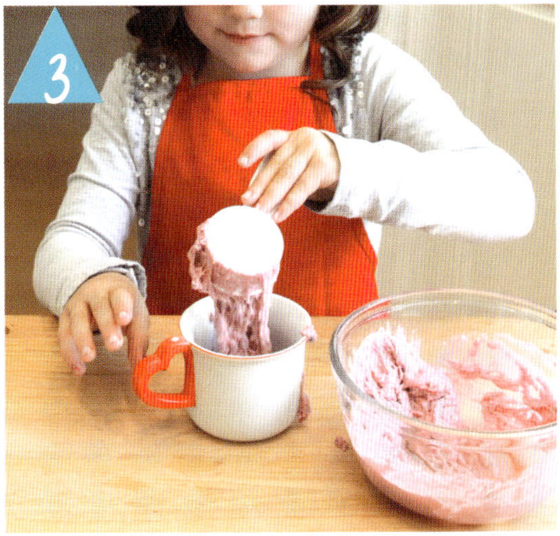
3

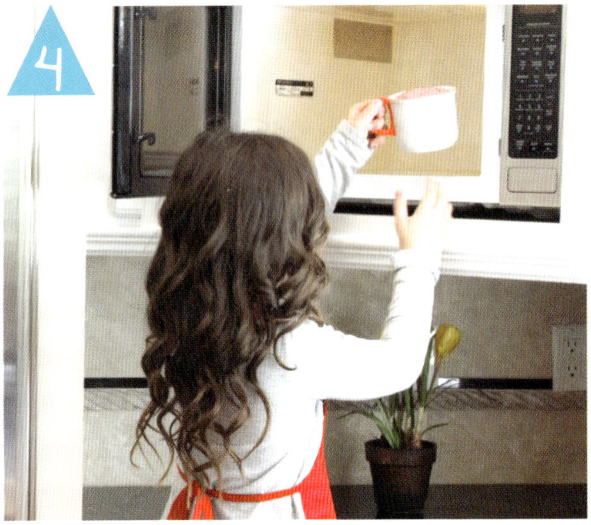
4

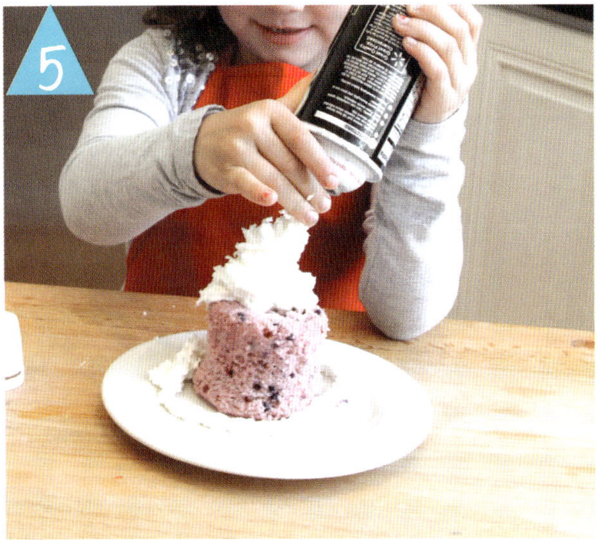
5

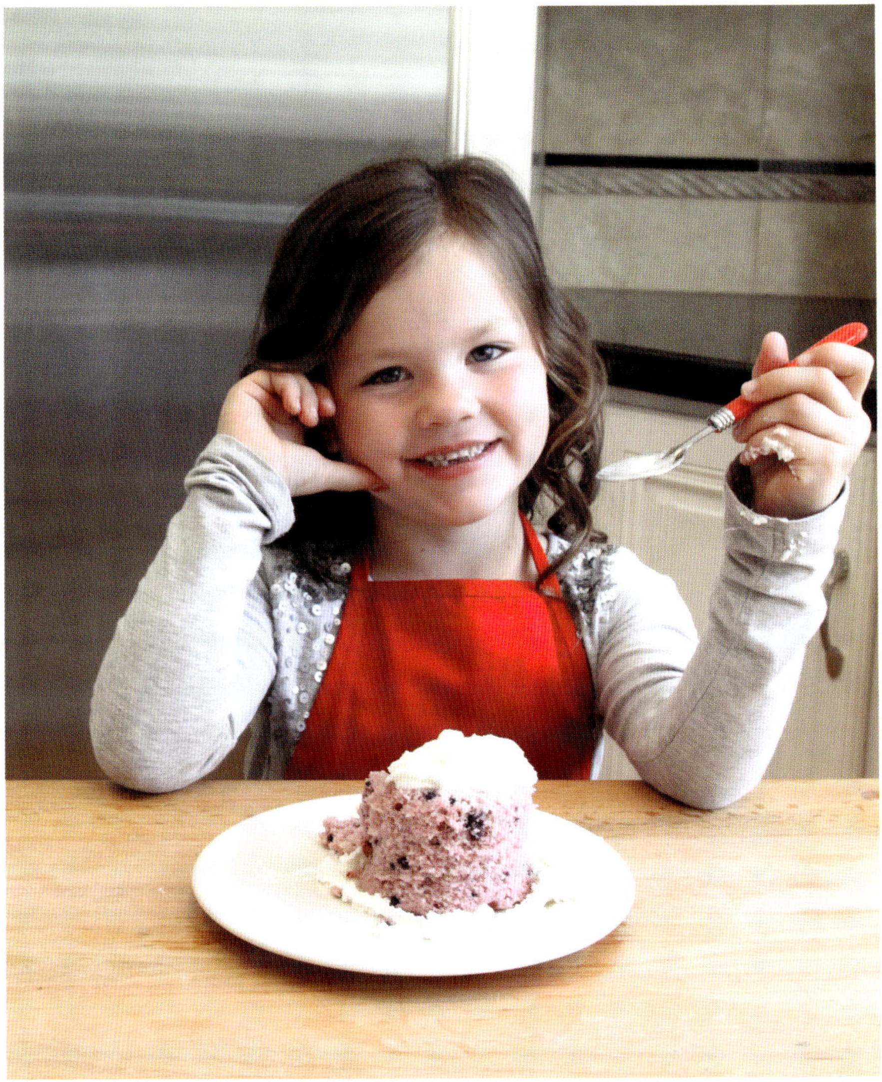

Grape Berry Muffin Cup

(serves 3-4)

DIRECTIONS

1. In a medium bowl, add the berry muffin mix and the grape juice (instead of water the mix calls for).
2. Stir the mixture until it is smooth.
3. Pour ½ cup of the mixture into a large mug.
4. Microwave for 1½–2 minutes.
5. Take the mug out of the microwave carefully with hot pads. Turn the mug upside down over a plate. Give it a shake until the muffin falls out.
6. Add butter and whipped cream to top it off.

WHAT ELSE CAN YOU DO?

You can make blueberry muffins in a mug the same way. Just use a box of blueberry muffin mix. Follow the directions for the mix. After the mix is ready to bake, pour it into a mug, about half full. Cook for 1½–2 minutes in the microwave.

Level of difficulty: **MEDIUM**
(adult supervision for microwave)

KITCHEN TOOLS

microwave
microwave-safe mug
spoon
plate
hot pads

INGREDIENTS

berry muffin mix
1 cup grape juice
butter
whipped cream

FOOD GROUPS

Grains	flour
Fruit	berries
	grape juice
Dairy	whipped cream

Blue and Purple • 39

KITCHEN TOOLS

frying pan or electric skillet
spatula
medium bowl
measuring cup

INGREDIENTS

1 cup blueberries, rinsed
1 cup pancake mix
¾ cup water
cooking spray (olive oil or coconut oil are the healthiest)

FOOD GROUPS

Dairy	eggs
Grain	flour
Fruit	blueberries

Blueberry-licious Pancakes
(serves 3)

DIRECTIONS

1. In a medium mixing bowl, add the pancake mix and water.
2. Mix for about 3 minutes. You can look at the clock or set a timer.
3. Fold ½ cup of the rinsed blueberries into the mixture.
4. Spray a pan or an electric skillet with cooking spray.
5. Turn the heat on the stove or skillet to medium.
6. With a ladle, pour some of the pancake mixture onto the skillet. Any shape will do as you practice.
7. The mixture will quickly turn into a pancake. When you see little bubbles pop in the mixture, that means you can flip the pancake over to cook the other side.
8. Wait about 1 minute. Peek under the pancake with your pancake turner. If the bottom of the pancake is a light brown color, it's ready to take out of the pan and put on a plate. Pour on your favorite syrup or make some Orange Syrup Topping, which you can find in the orange section of this book.

WHAT ELSE CAN YOU DO?

Use coconut water to replace the water in the ingredients.

Use crushed pecans instead of blueberries.

Level of difficulty: **HARD**
(adult supervision for stove or electric skillet)

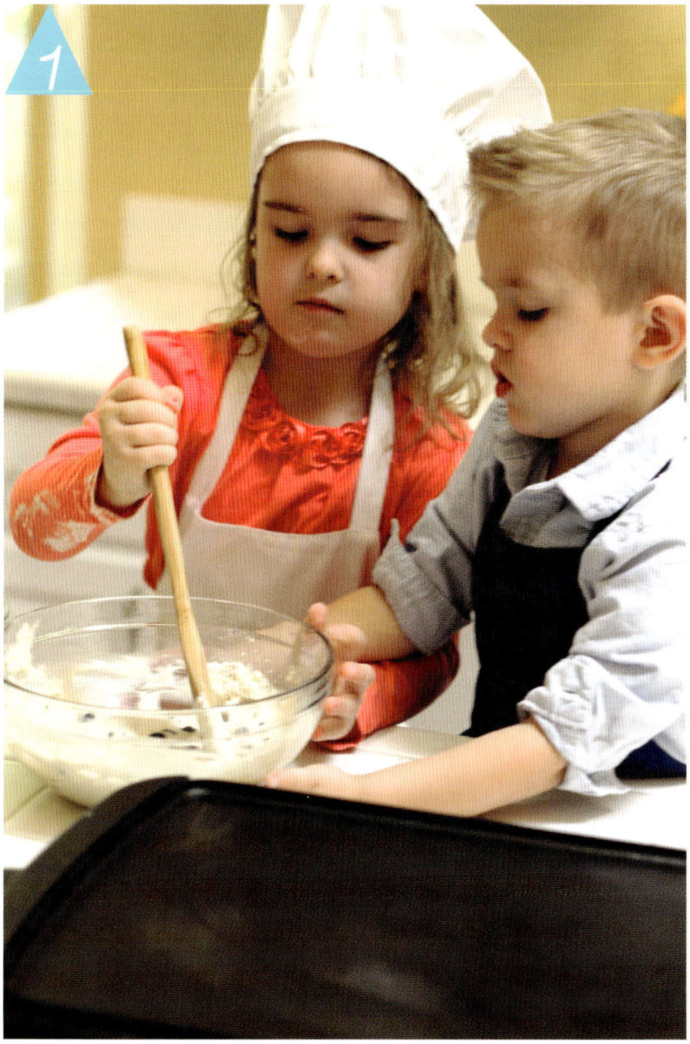
1
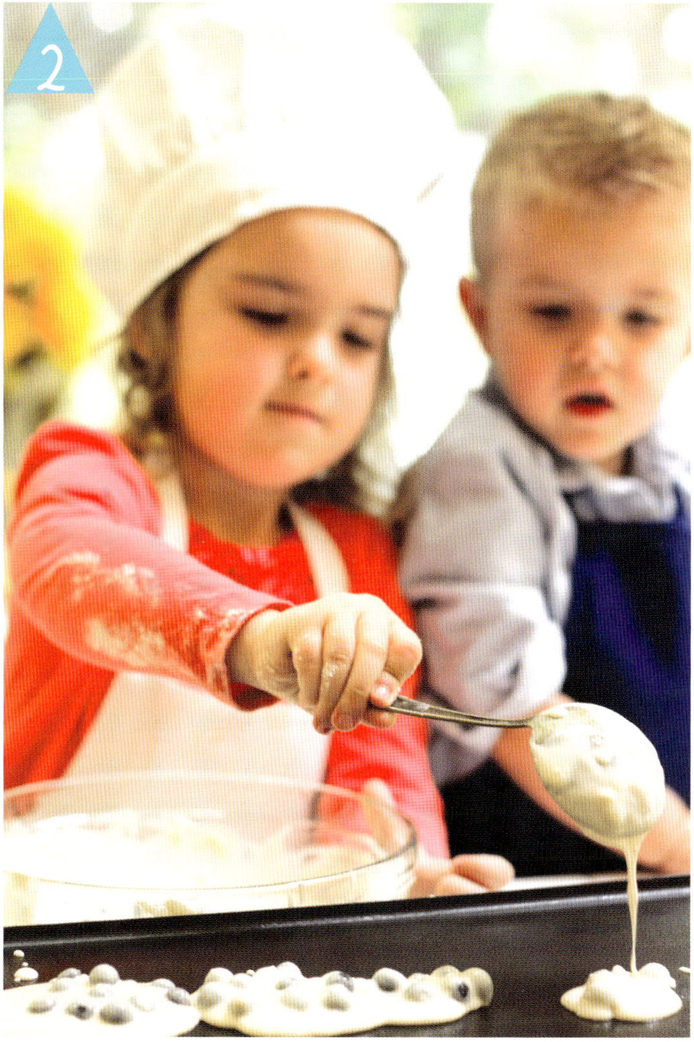
2
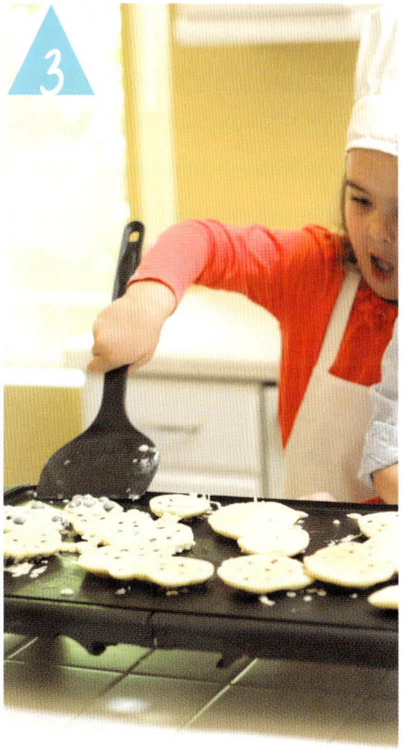
3
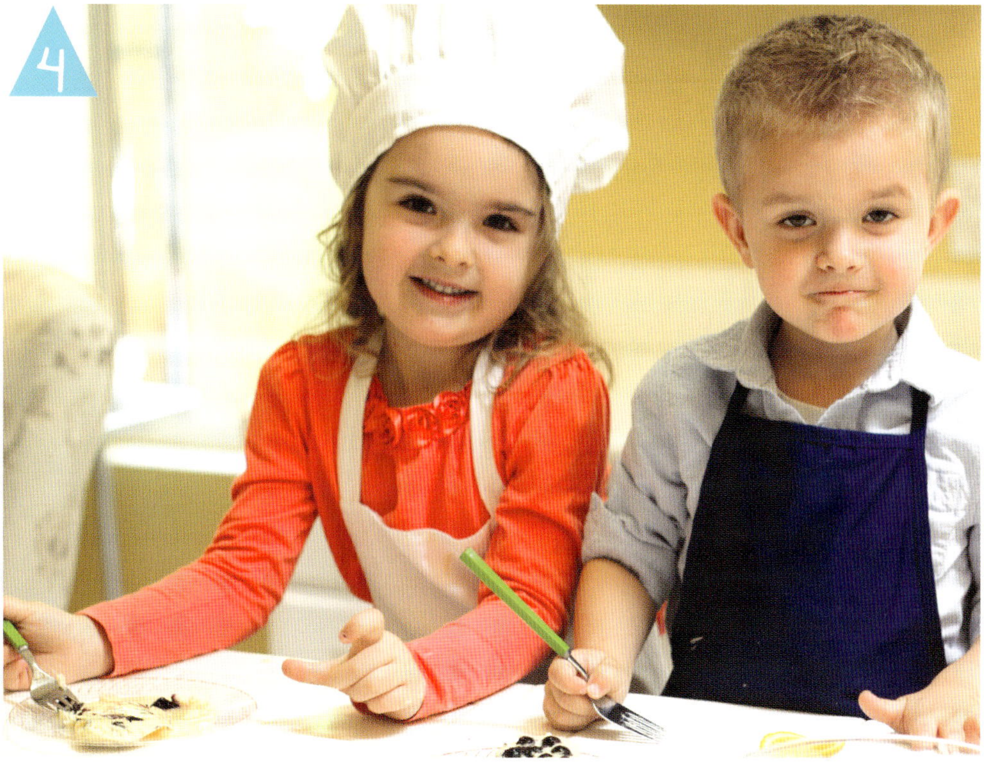
4

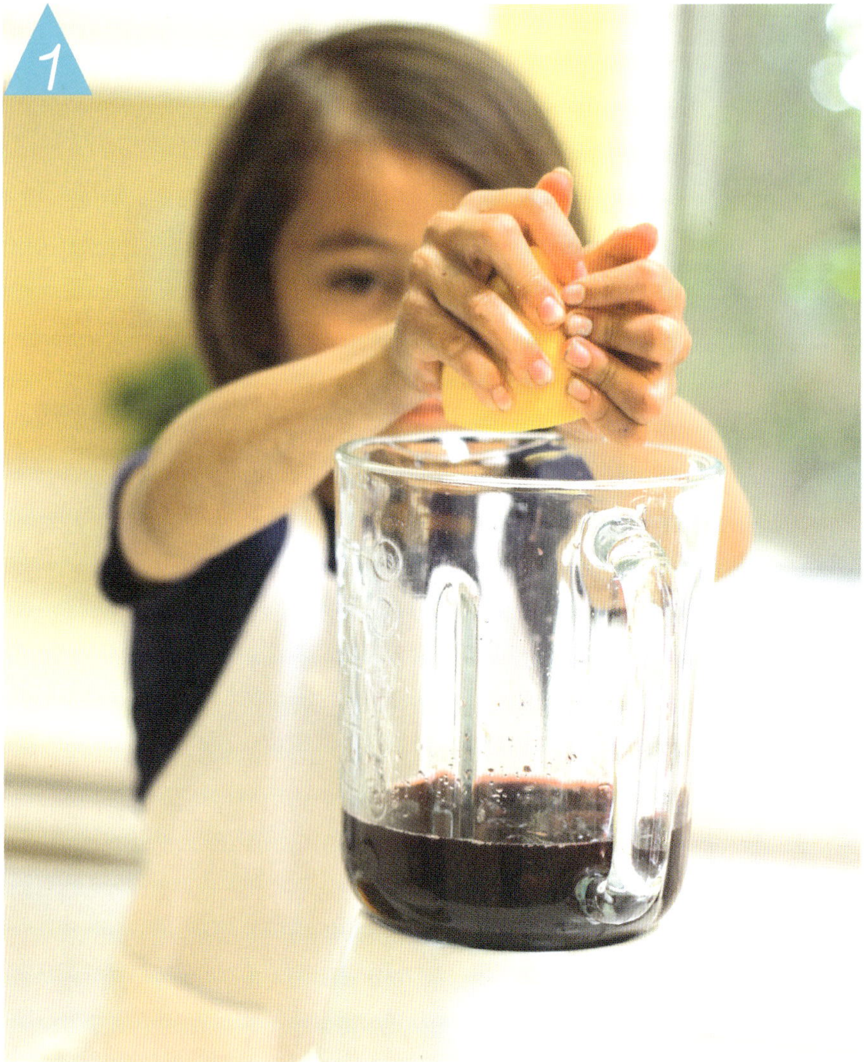
1
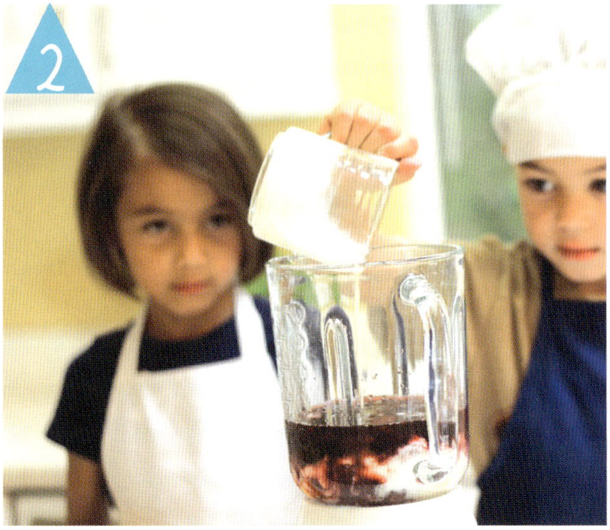
2
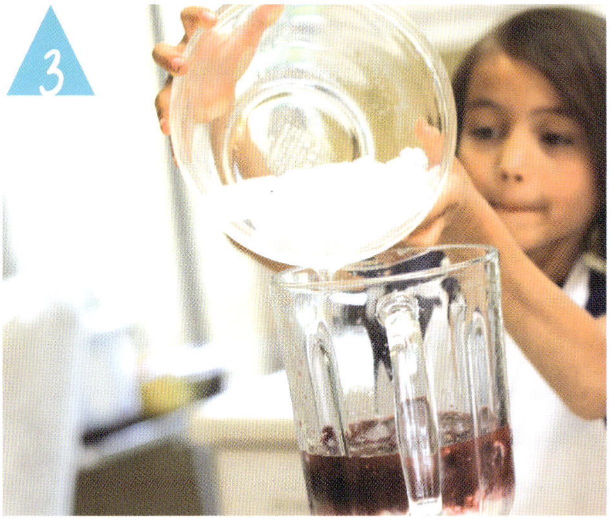
3
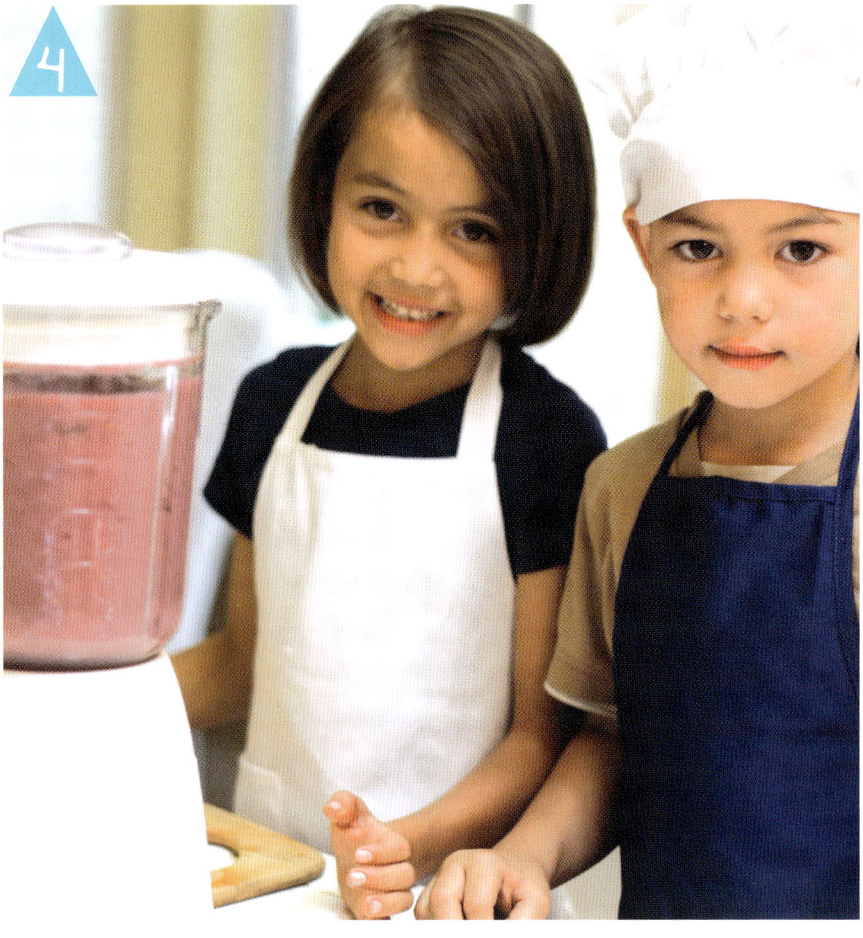
4
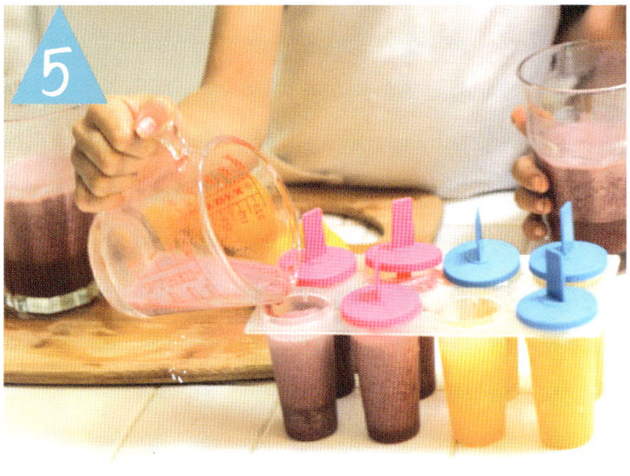
5
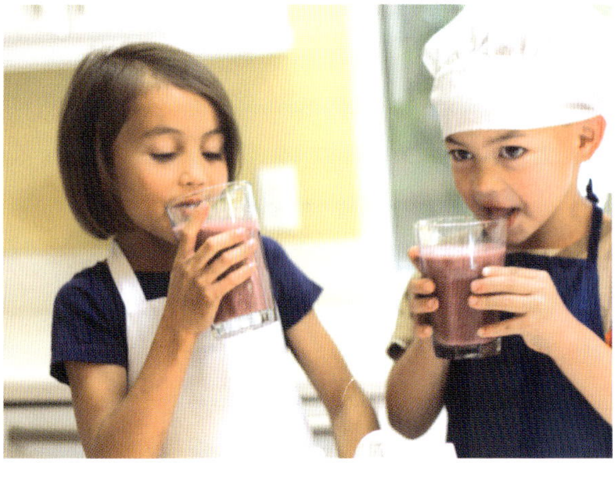

Berry Swirl Slush
(serves 4)

DIRECTIONS

1. Add the grape juice and blackberries to a blender.
2. Squeeze the juice from ½ of an orange into the blender and add the other ingredients.
3. Blend the ingredients on high for 10 seconds. Or count to 10 slowly.
4. Pour the juice mixture over ice in a glass and drink up!
5. If you want to make popsicles, pour the mixture into a popsicle container and freeze for several hours. To get the frozen pops out easier put the frozen container upside down under hot tap water for about 40 seconds. Turn it over and see if the popsicles pull out of the container easily. If not, repeat for an additional 10 seconds and try again.

WHAT ELSE CAN YOU DO?

Put the juice made from the blender in a plastic container. Freeze for 3 hours. Take it out and let it warm on the counter for 20 minutes. Then put it in bowls and eat.

Put other kinds of juice in the frozen pop holder to make a variety of colors.

Level of difficulty: EASY
(supervision for blender and cutting orange)

KITCHEN TOOLS

blender
measuring cup

INGREDIENTS

½ cup 100% grape juice
½ cup fresh blackberries
1 orange, cut in half
½ cup milk
3 Tbsp. agave or cane sugar
2 cups ice

FOOD GROUPS

Fruit	blackberries grape juice orange
Dairy	milk

Blue and Purple • 43

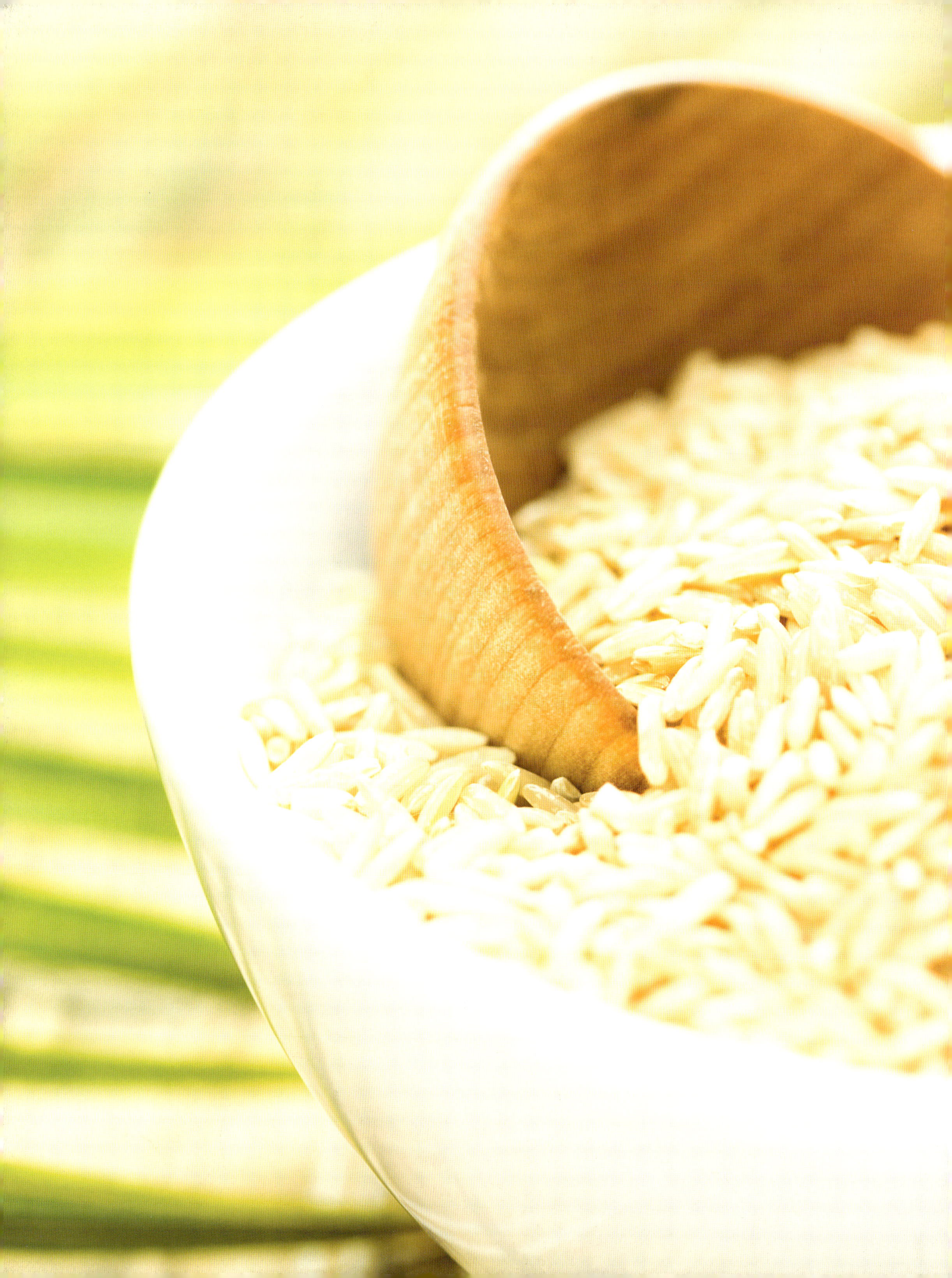

BROWN

1
2
3
4

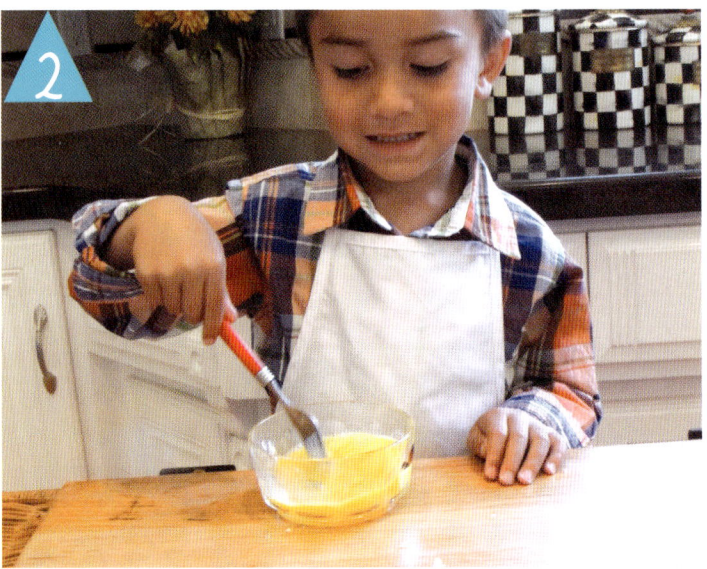

Soy Good Fried Rice

(serves 2)

DIRECTIONS

1. Put the frozen vegetables in a small bowl and microwave for 1 minute. Put this bowl aside.
2. Crack the egg in a bowl or cup. Put it in microwave for 30 seconds. Make sure it has cooked completely. If it hasn't, cook it for 10 more seconds.
3. Put the cooked egg on your cutting board. Smash it a little as it is cooling. After it has cooled, cut it into small bits.
4. With adult supervision: Put the pan on the stove. Add the oil. Add the veggies. Let it cook on low as you stir it around in the oil. Add the cooked rice. Stir it around. Add the egg. Add the soy sauce.
5. Stir it around for a minute or two to absorb the soy sauce and oil. This is called stir-fry because you stir the ingredients around as you fry them in a pan. And it's fried rice because it is fried on the stove.
6. Turn off the stove. Let it cool for about 5 minutes. Now you can scoop the fried rice out of the pan into a bowl. Be sure to use a hot pad if the handle is hot. And never touch the main part of the pan.

WHAT ELSE CAN YOU DO?

Add chicken or beef. This will add more protein.

Level of difficulty: **HARD**
(adult supervision for stove and cutting)

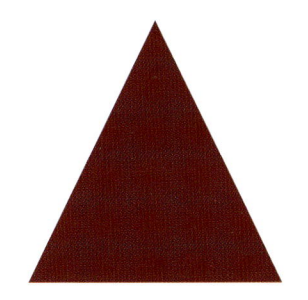

KITCHEN TOOLS

frying pan
spatula
spoon
small microwave-safe bowl
small microwave-safe mug
butter knife
cutting board
plate
spoon or chopsticks

INGREDIENTS

¼ cup frozen peas and carrots
1 egg
½ Tbsp. sesame oil
1¼ cups cooked brown rice
2 Tbsp. soy sauce

FOOD GROUPS

Grains	rice
Vegetables	peas
	carrots
Protein	peas
	egg

Brown o 47

Apple Crisp Cups
(serves 2)

KITCHEN TOOLS

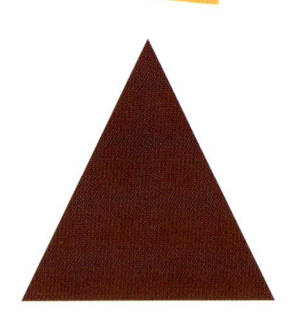

2 plastic cups
spoon
small ziploc bag
rolling pin or ice cream scoop to crush granola bars

INGREDIENTS

1 hard, crunchy granola bar (pkg. will have 2)
1 cup applesauce
1 small yogurt—your favorite flavor

FOOD GROUPS

Grains	granola
Fruit	applesauce
Dairy	yogurt

DIRECTIONS

1. Break the granola bars into chunks.
2. Put these chunks into a baggie. Crush them with something hard, like a rolling pin or ice cream scoop.
3. Put a layer of applesauce in a cup. Add a layer of yogurt.
4. Add a layer of the crushed granola bar.
5. Repeat the layers until each cup is full.

WHAT ELSE CAN YOU DO?

You can use flavored granola or granola cereal.

Level of difficulty: **EASY**

1

2

3

Vanilla Warm Fuzzies Drink

(serves 1)

KITCHEN TOOLS

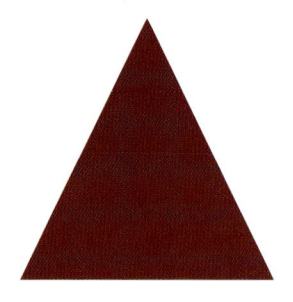

microwave-safe mug
spoon
teaspoon

INGREDIENTS

3/4 cup almond milk
1/8 tsp. Cinnamon
1/8 tsp. vanilla
2 tsp. agave or cane sugar

FOOD GROUPS

Grain | almond milk

DIRECTIONS

1. In a mug, add almond milk until the cup is a little more than half full.
2. Shake some cinnamon in the cup.
3. Add sugar and vanilla.
4. Put the mug in a microwave for 80 seconds.
5. Take it out carefully. Put a spoon in the warm fuzzy to test for temperature.

WHAT SHOULD YOU KNOW?

When you drink a warm or hot drink, you sip it slowly.

WHAT ELSE CAN YOU DO?

Use milk instead of almond milk.

50 • Wick

Level of difficulty: MEDIUM
(adult supervision for microwave)

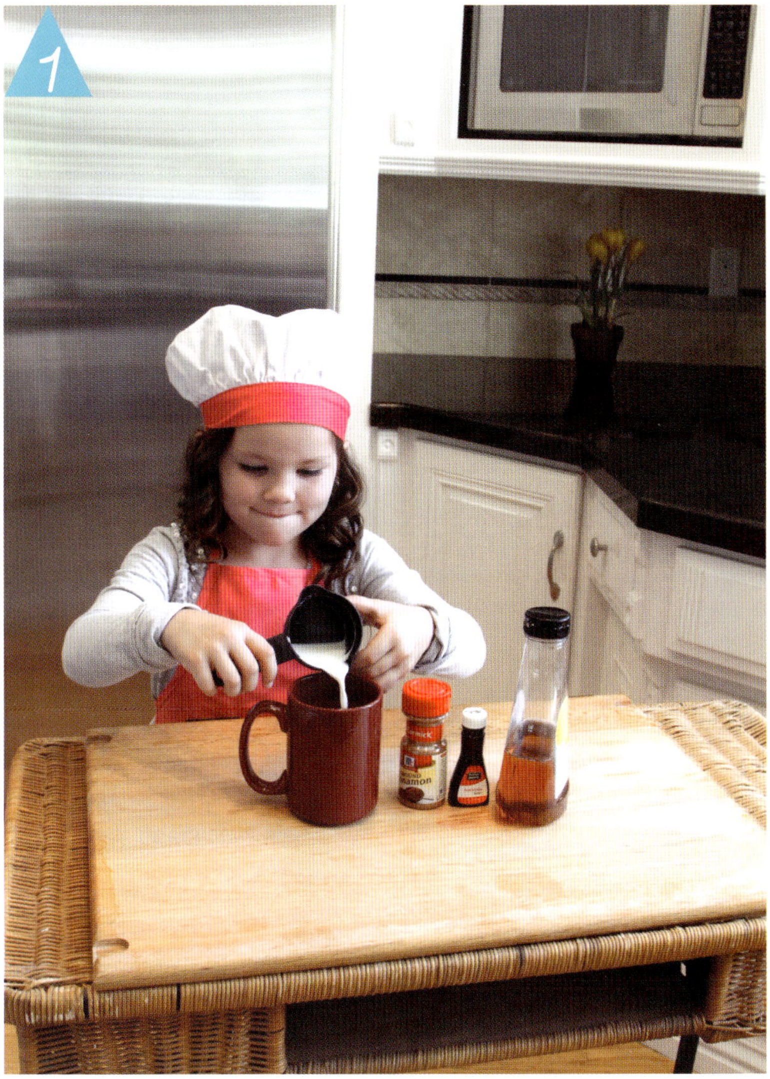
1

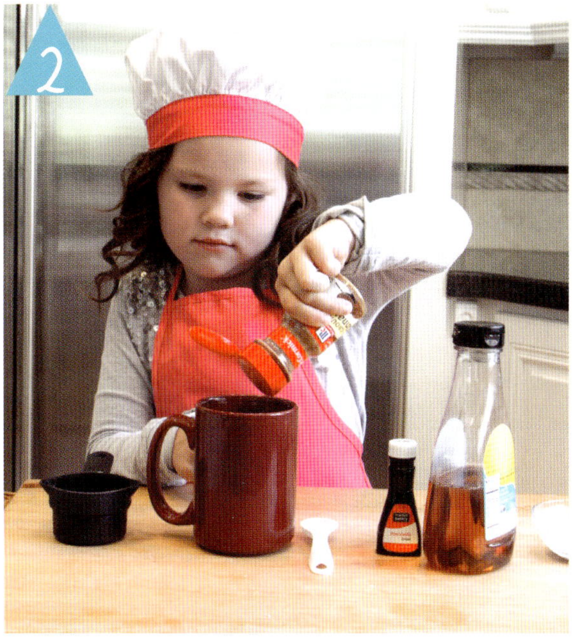
2

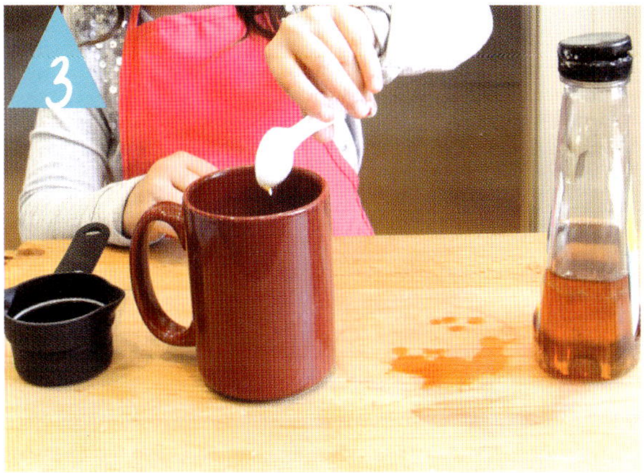
3

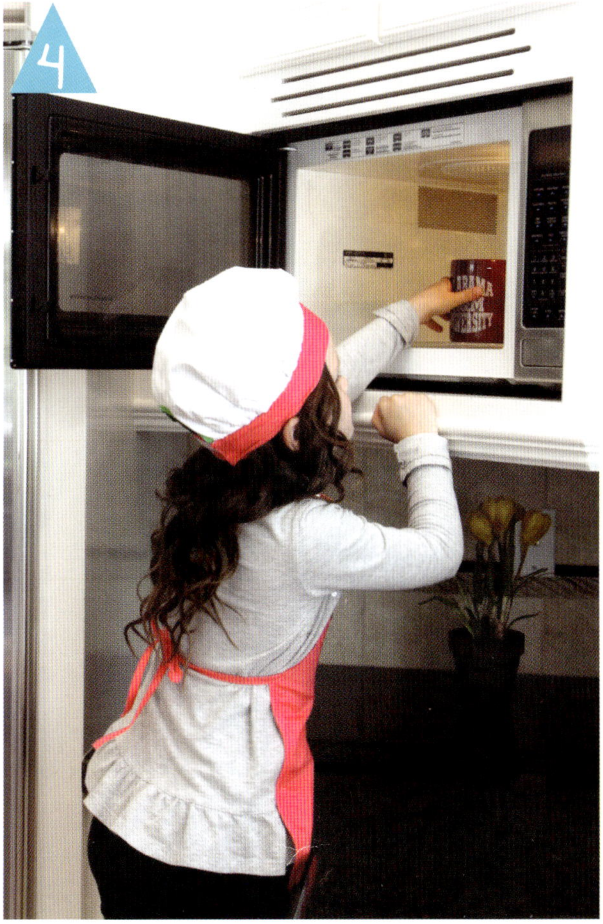
4

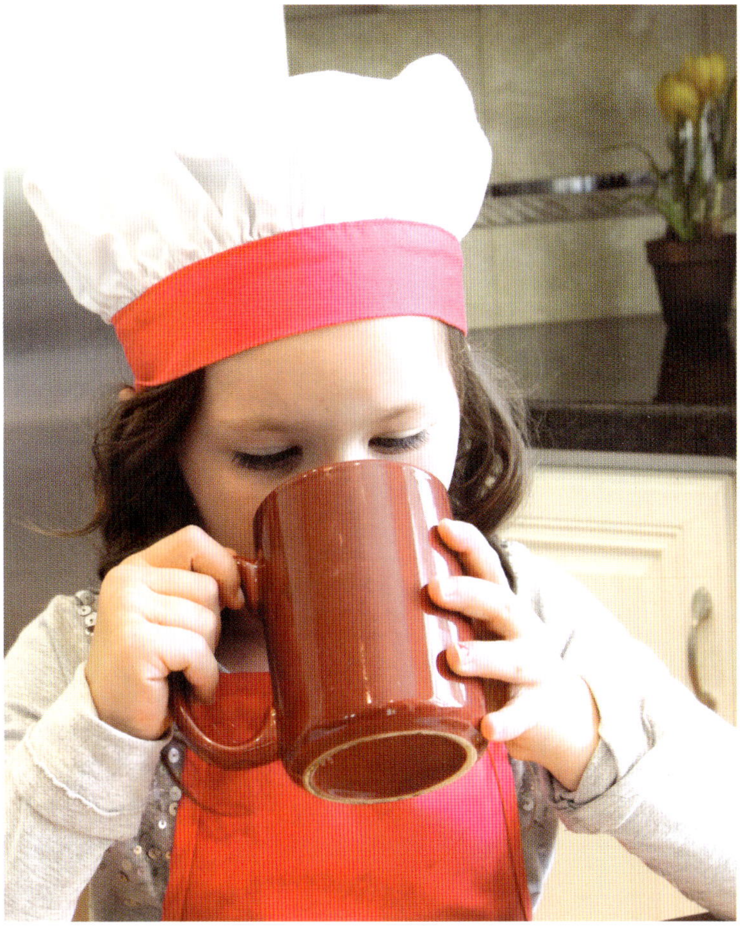

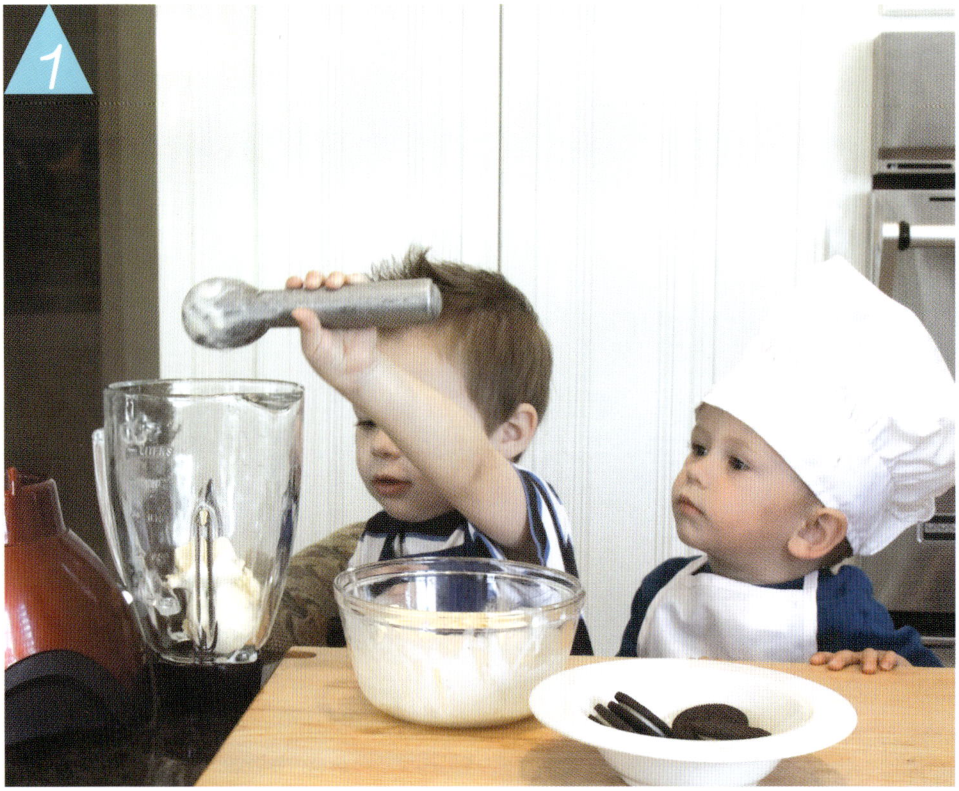
1

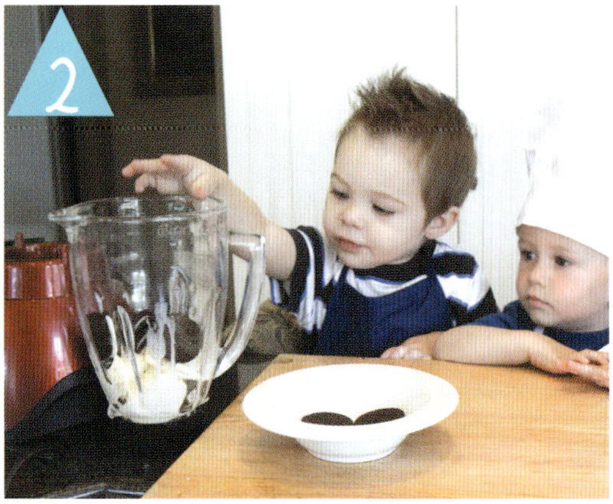
2

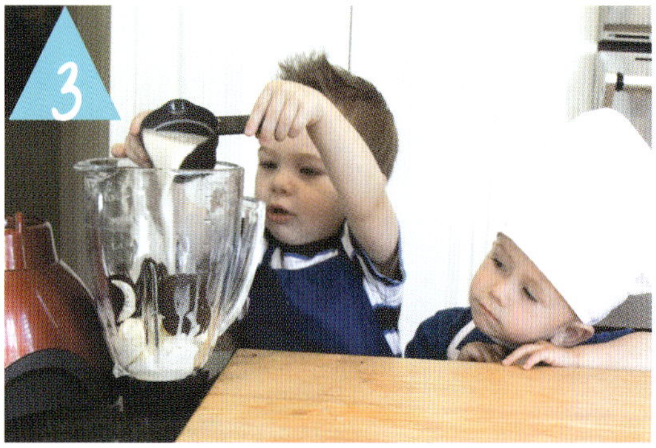
3

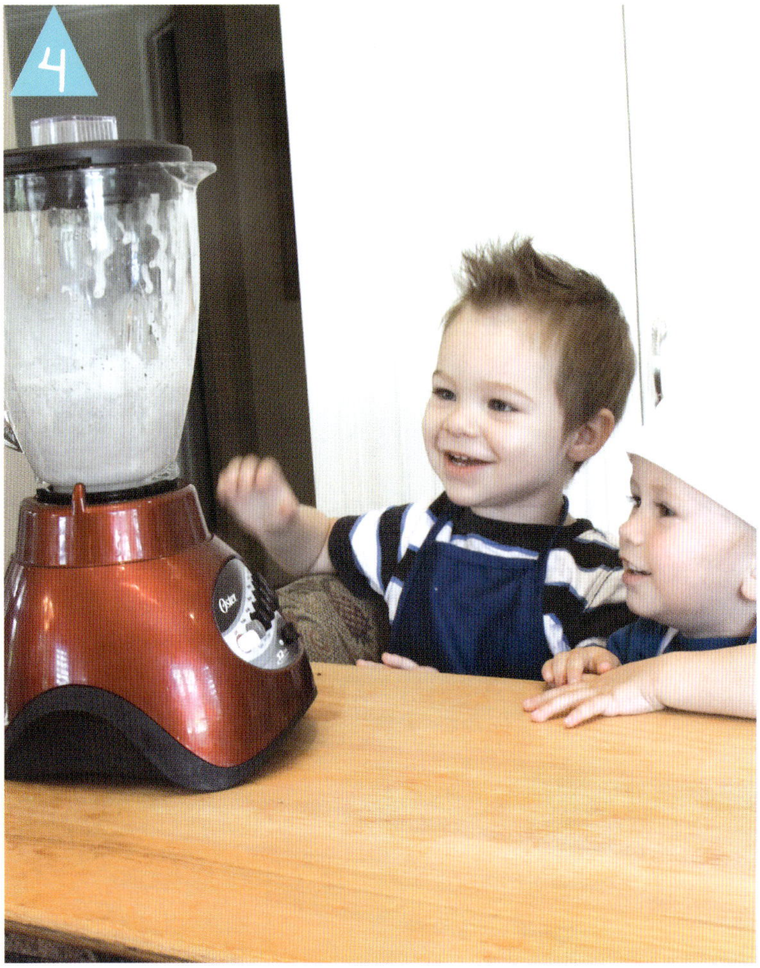
4

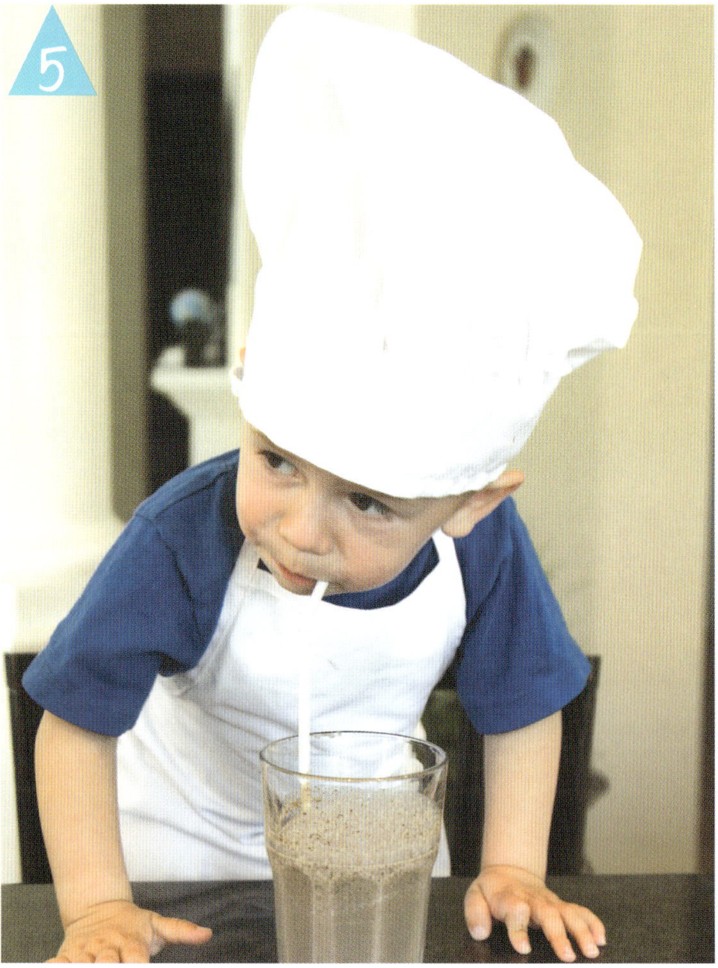
5

Double Trouble Dirt Shake
(serves 2)

DIRECTIONS

1. Put the ice cream in a blender.
2. Add the almond milk.
3. Add the Oreos to the blender.
4. Mix on low speed for 5 seconds.
5. Stop the blender and pour the shake into a cup.

WHAT ELSE CAN YOU DO?

You can use soy or coconut ice cream. You can use other crunchy cookies instead of Oreos.

WHAT CAN GO WRONG?

If the shake is not thick enough, add ½ to 1 cup of ice to the blender with the mixture. Blend it on high for 2 minutes. That will thicken it.

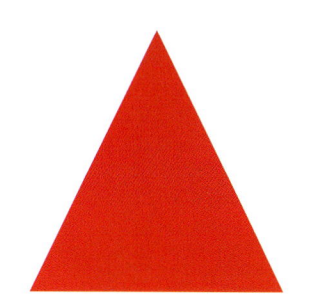

Level of difficulty: EASY
(adult supervision of blender)

KITCHEN TOOLS

ice cream scoop
blender
measuring cup

INGREDIENTS

5 Oreos
½ cup almond milk
4 scoops vanilla ice cream

FOOD GROUP

| Protein | almond milk |
| Dairy | ice cream |

Brown o 53

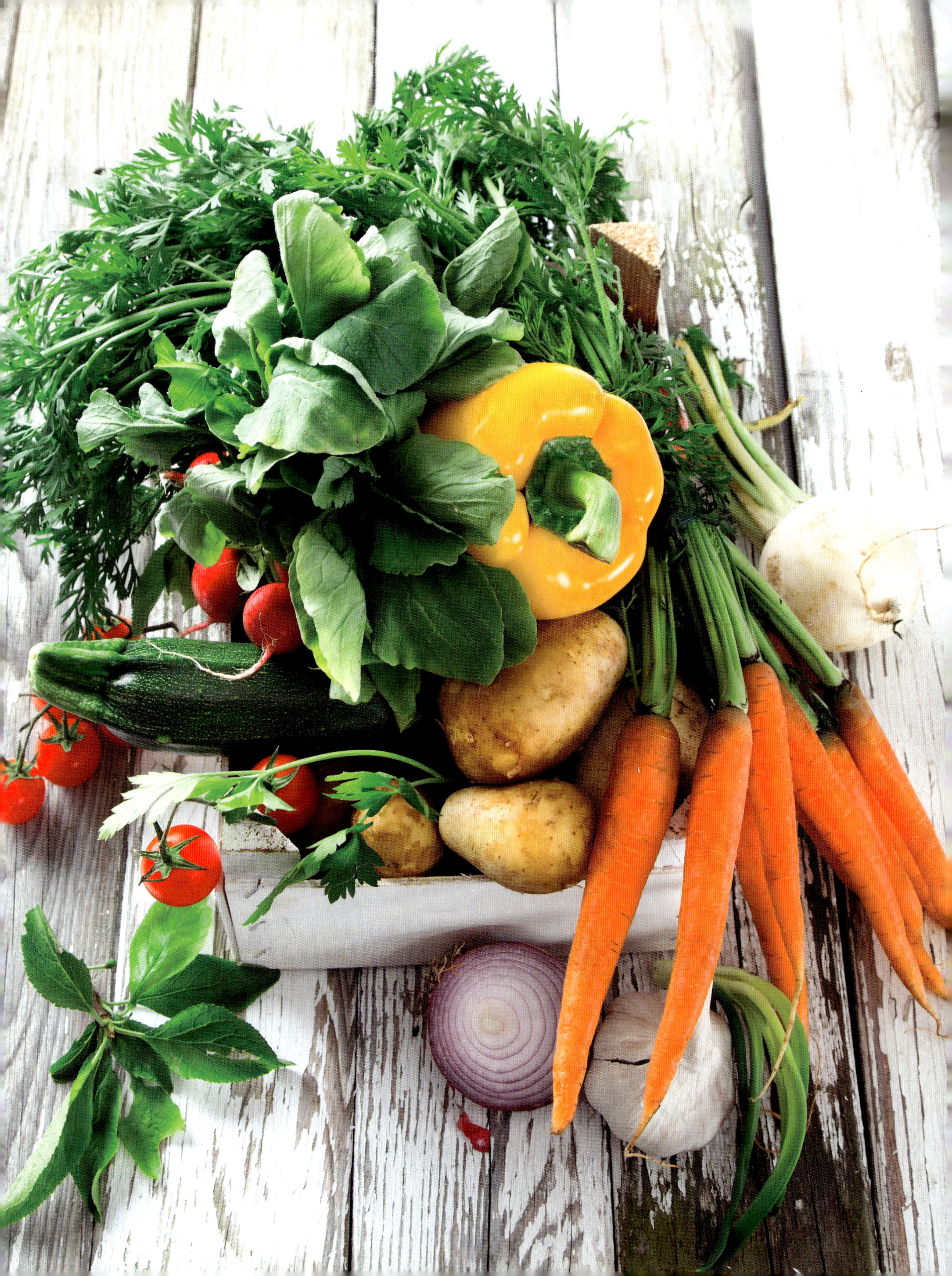

COLORFUL FOODS

Colorful Tortilla Wrap
(serves 1)

DIRECTIONS

1. Put the tortilla on a plate.
2. With a butter knife, spread the mayonnaise or ranch dressing on the tortilla.
3. Add the cheese and meat.
4. Add the baby spinach, tomatoes, olives, or other veggies.
5. Fold the tortilla up from the bottom. Fold it in on each side.
6. Eat up!

WHAT ELSE CAN YOU DO?

You can use other favorite vegetables to the tortilla wrap. Think of vegetables you'd eat in a sub sandwich.

KITCHEN TOOLS

plate
butter knife
cutting board

INGREDIENTS

1 tortilla (photo shows green spinach tortilla)
mayonnaise or ranch dressing
2 slices cheese
2 thin slices deli meat
spinach
tomatoes, chopped
olives, chopped

FOOD GROUPS

Grain	tortilla
Vegetable	tomatoes
	spinach
	olives
Protein	deli meat

56 o Wick

Level of difficulty: **EASY**
(adult supervision of cutting)

1

2

3

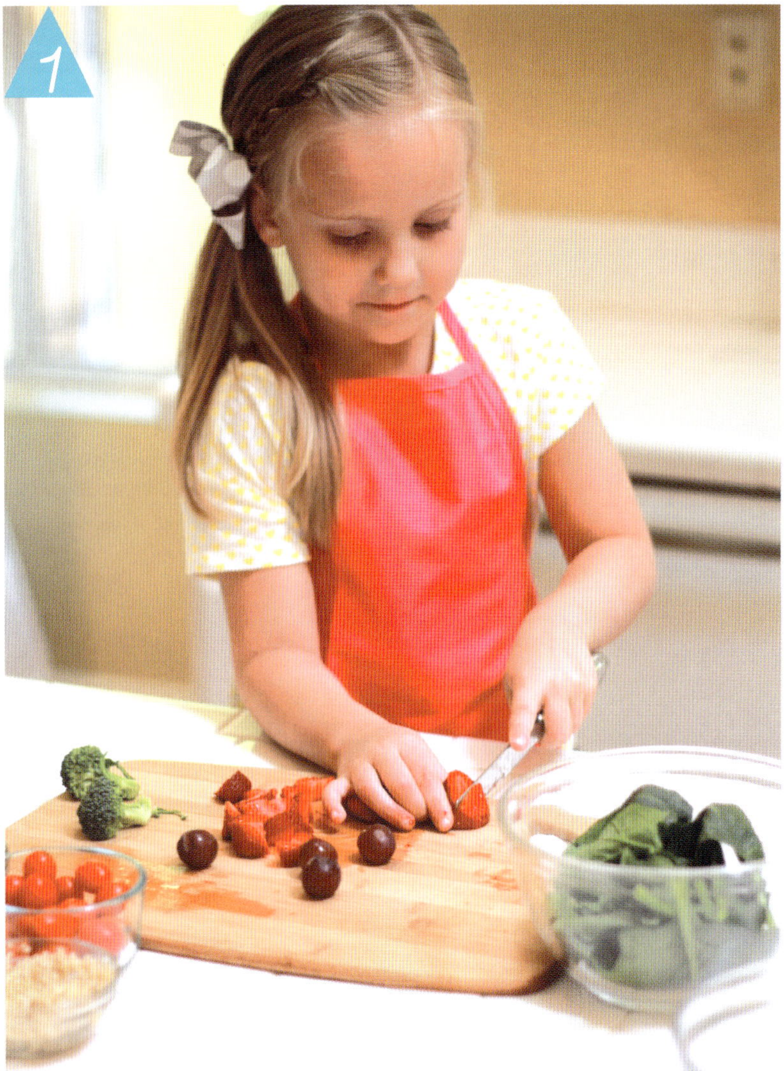
1

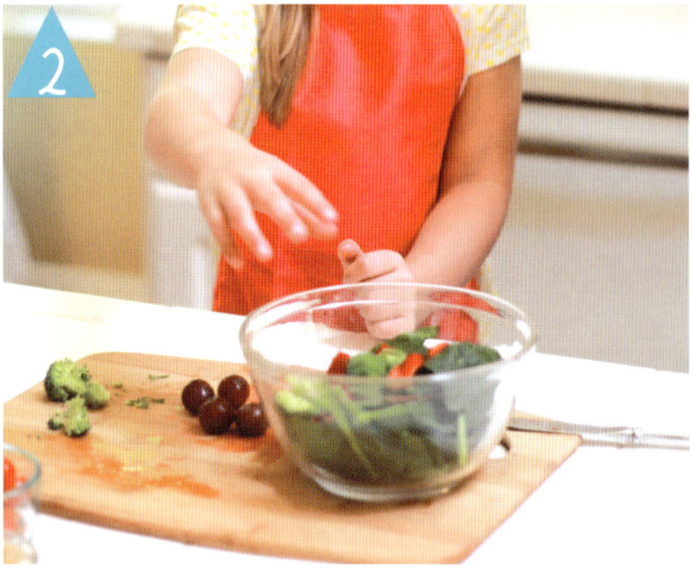
2

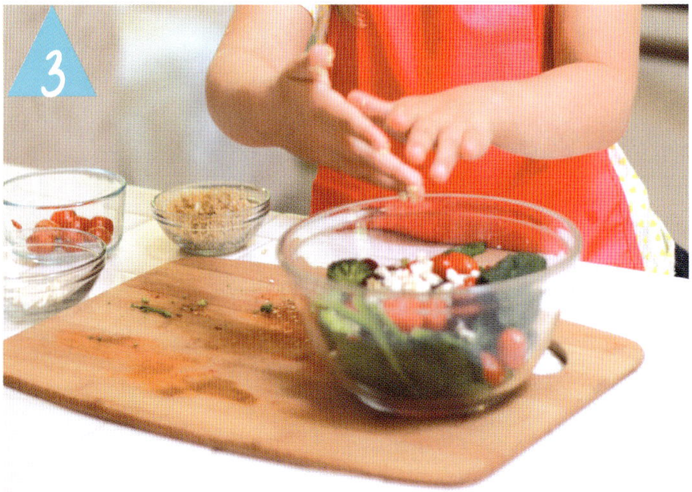
3

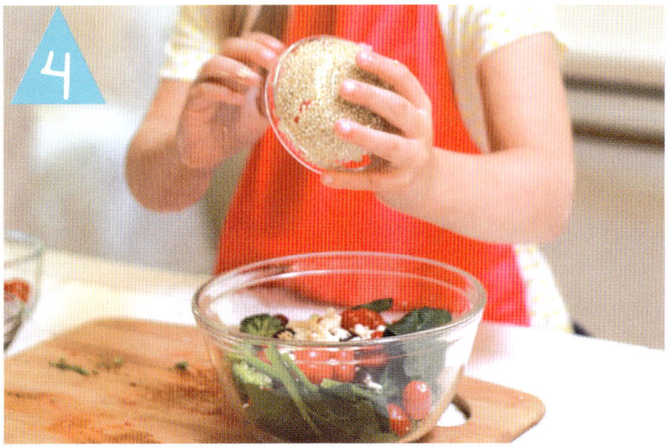
4

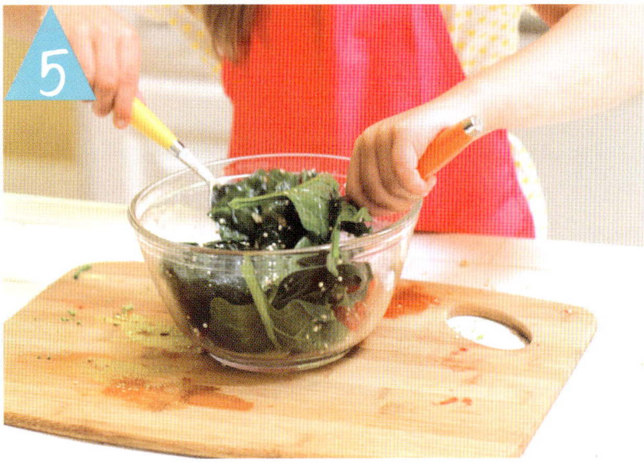
5

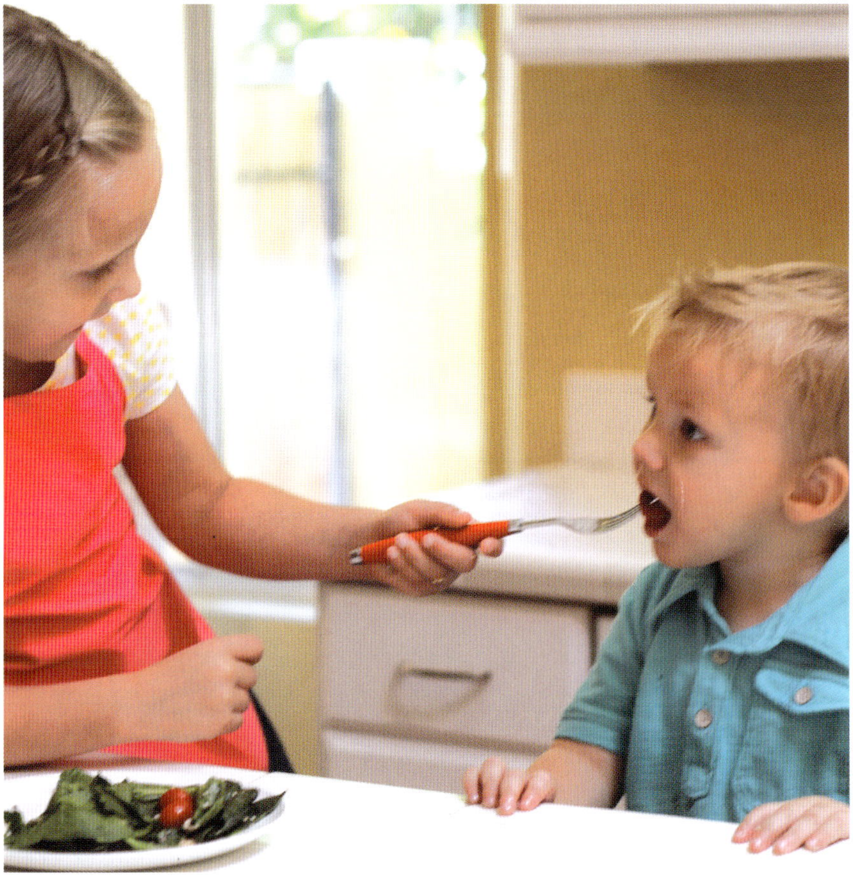

Colorful Sassy Salad
(serves 1)

DIRECTIONS

1. Wash the fruit and lettuce in a colander.
2. Cut the green stems and leaves off of the strawberries.
3. Put the spinach leaves in a salad bowl. Add cut up strawberries.
4. Add the blueberries and feta cheese.
5. Add the quinoa to the salad. Pour on your favorite dressing.
6. Mix the salad well with salad fork and spoon, and it's ready to eat!

Level of difficulty: EASY
(adult supervision of cutting)

KITCHEN TOOLS

colander
cutting board
knife
salad bowl
measuring cups

INGREDIENTS

1 cup spinach leaves, rinsed
3 strawberries
1/3 cup blueberries
1/4 cup feta cheese
1/8 cup quinoa, cooked and cooled
chicken, cooked and diced (optional)
your favorite dressing (I prefer a sweet Italian dressing)

FOOD GROUPS

Grain	quinoa
Vegetable	spinach leaves
Fruit	blueberries strawberries
Protein	quinoa chicken
Dairy	Cheese

Colorful o 59

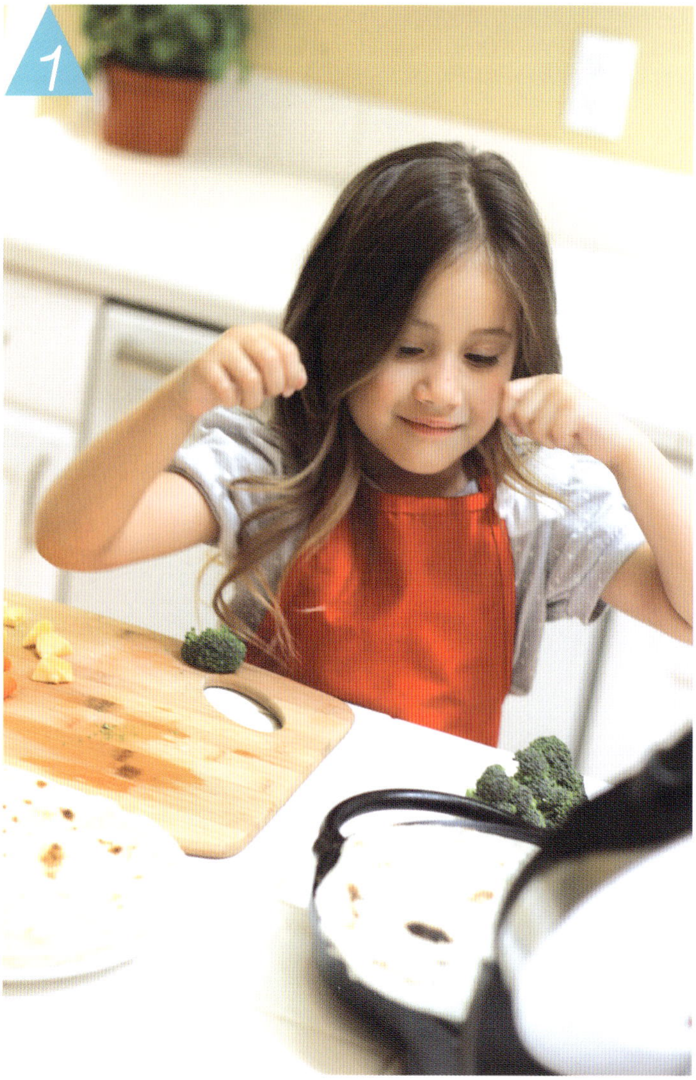
1

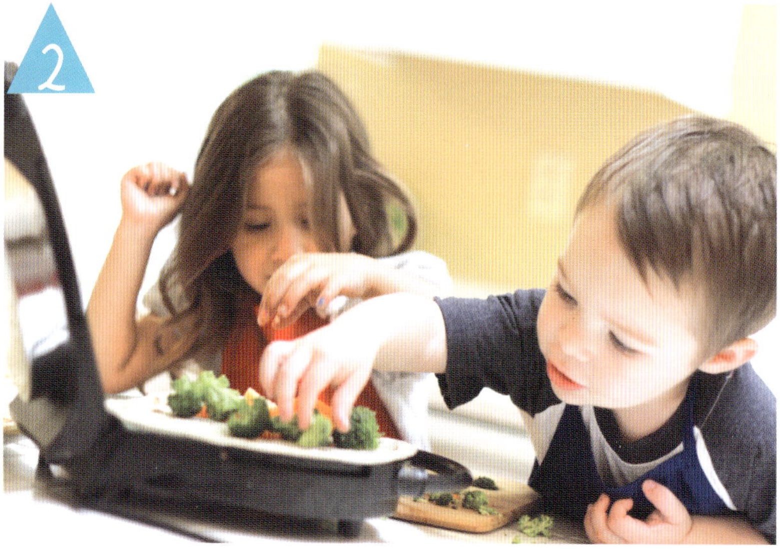
2

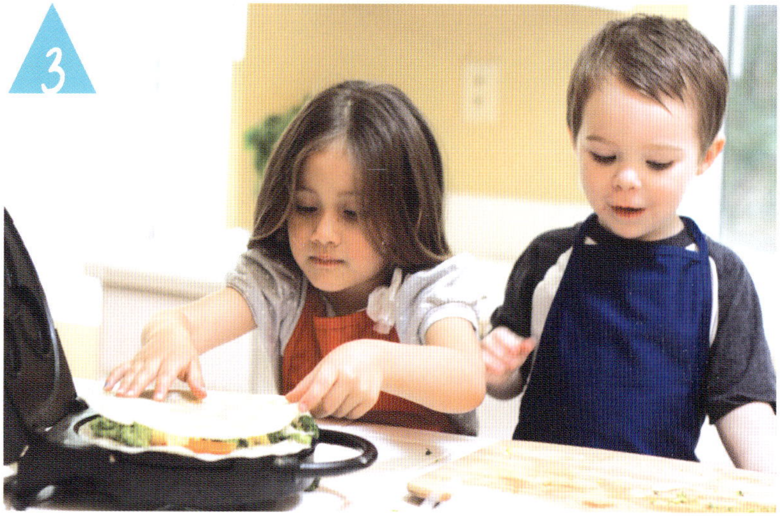
3

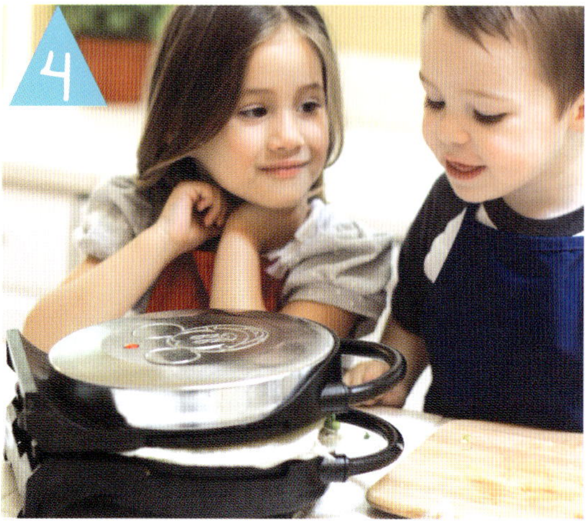
4

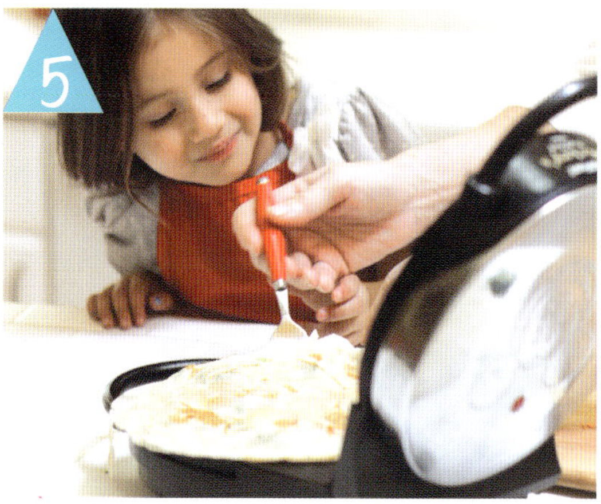
5

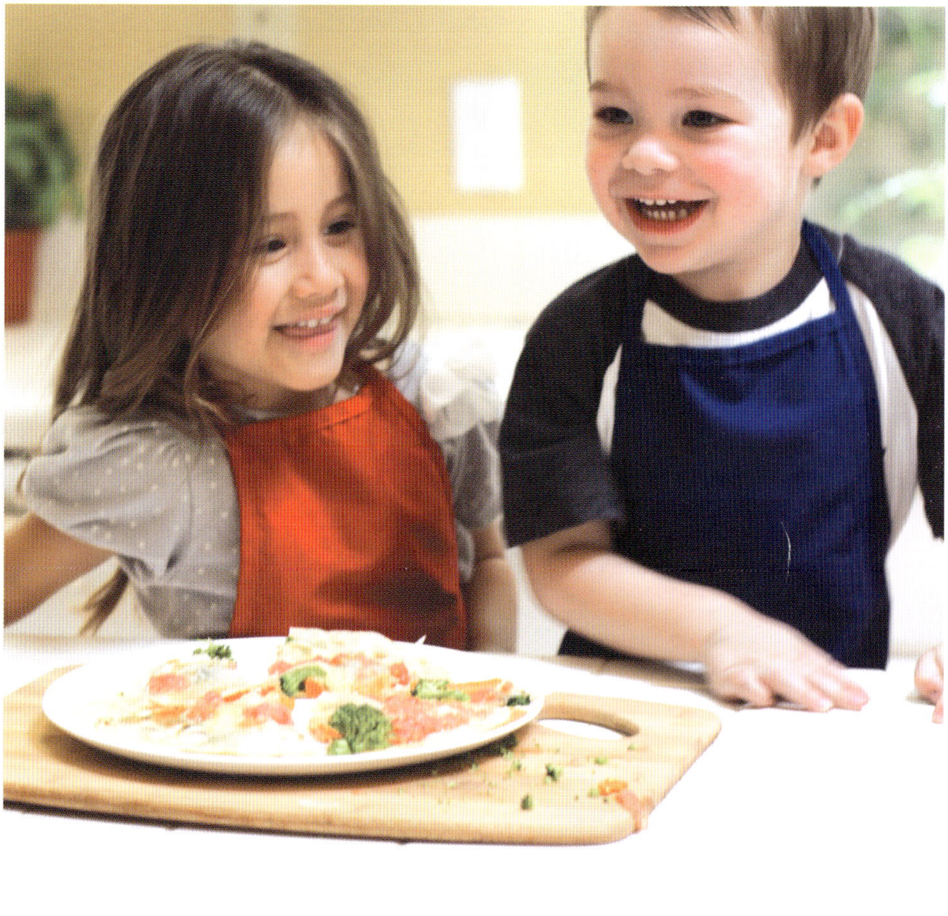

Colorful Waffle Quesadilla

(serves 2)

DIRECTIONS

1. Cut the broccoli and carrots into thin pieces. Cut the cheese into thin pieces, too, if you don't have shredded cheese.
2. Plug in a waffle iron.
3. While the waffle iron is warming up, open the waffle iron and carefully lay a tortilla on top.
4. On top of the tortilla, place the pieces of cheese and vegetables.
5. Place a second tortilla on top of the vegetables and cheese. Close the top of the waffle iron. The top may not close all the way, since this quesadilla is thicker than a waffle. That is okay—it's still heating and cooking your tortilla.
6. Don't pay attention to the light on the waffle maker. That is only for a waffle. Wait about two minutes. Open the waffle iron and check to see if the tortilla is lightly brown on the bottom. Do this carefully. The inside of the waffle iron is hot.
7. When its brown enough on both sides, carefully take the quesadilla off the waffle iron with a spatula or a large spoon. Move it to a plate.

WHAT ELSE CAN YOU DO?

Eat this with homemade salsa or shredded lettuce and cut-up tomatoes.

Level of difficulty: HARD
(adult supervision of waffle maker, cutting)

KITCHEN TOOLS

knife
cutting board
waffle iron

INGREDIENTS

4 tortillas
8 baby carrots
1 bunch broccoli
1 cup shredded cheese (or cheese cut into small pieces)

FOOD GROUPS

Grains	tortilla
Vegetable	broccoli
	carrots
Dairy	cheese

KITCHEN TOOLS

microwave-safe small bowl
microwave-safe medium bowl
large spoon

INGREDIENTS

1 cup small elbow macaroni
(or your favorite pasta)
½ cup shredded cheese (or ½
cup of your favorite cheese
cut in small pieces)
¼ baby spinach
¼ cup carrot
⅛ cup cooked quinoa
⅛ cup cooked and shredded
chicken
⅛ tsp. butter
⅛ tsp. salt

FOOD GROUPS

Grains	macaroni quinoa
Vegetables	carrots spinach
Protein	quinoa chicken
Dairy	cheese

62 o Wick

Colorful Mac and Cheese
(serves 2)

DIRECTIONS

1. Add the macaroni to a medium microwave-safe bowl filled with 4 cups of water. Add a little bit of butter and salt.
2. Stir it 3 times.
3. Microwave the macaroni in the bowl for five minutes. Stir. Heat for 3 more minutes. If the macaroni is still too hard, let it sit for a few minutes in the bowl of hot water. Make sure you have adult supervision for this step.
4. With oven mitts, pour the macaroni and water into a colander or strainer to drain the water. Be careful and hold your face back from the sink—the steam from the water is hot.
5. Put the cooked macaroni in a small bowl. Add cheese and mix. You can use the powdered cheese mix if you are using a box of macaroni and cheese.
6. Stir the cheese into the macaroni until it is blended. (Taste test to see if you want just a little salt. The cheese is salty so it should be fine without salt.)
7. Add the shredded chicken, baby spinach, and carrots.
8. Add the cooked quinoa to the mixture and stir.
9. The type of cheese you use may make this stringier than boxed macaroni and cheese. Kids seem to think it's fun to eat.

WHAT ELSE CAN YOU DO?

Use a different kind of vegetables, like broccoli or peas. Use a different kind of cheese.

HOW CAN I MAKE THIS EASIER?

Use a macaroni & cheese box mix. Follow the directions on box, and then add vegetables, chicken, and quinoa.

Level of difficulty: **HARD**
(adult supervision for microwave and cutting)

1
2
3
4
5

INDEX

RED

STRAWBERRY SHORTCAKE CREPES 2
FIESTA SALSA 5
CHOCOLATE STRAWBERRY DIPS 7
MANGO BERRY SELTZER 8

ORANGE

CINNAMON SWEET POTATO FRIES 12
ORANGE CHOCOLATE CHIP COOKIES 15
BUNNY HOP FLOAT 16
CREAMY ORANGE SYRUP 19

YELLOW

READY SET GO CORN ON A STICK 23
FROZEN PINEAPPLE FLUFF 24
BANANA SPLIT CUPS 26

GREEN

ZESTY EDAMAME 31
FROSTY ZUCCHINI CUPCAKES 32
AWESOME AVOCADO SPREAD 34

BLUE

GRAPE BERRY MUFFIN CUP 39
BLUEBERRY-LICIOUS PANCAKES 40
BERRY SWIRL SLUSH 43

BROWN

SOY GOOD FRIED RICE 47
APPLE CRISP CUPS 48
VANILLA WARM FUZZIES DRINK 50
DOUBLE TROUBLE DIRT SHAKE 53

COLORFUL

COLORFUL TORTILLA WRAP 56
COLORFUL SASSY SALAD 59
COLORFUL WAFFLE QUESADILLA 61
COLORFUL MAC AND CHEESE 62

Index o 65

ACKNOWLEDGMENTS

My blessings have been ones of beauty and love as have I focused in on doing good in the world with this recipe book. Life changes were made at the same time I was working on this book. I started the book in Arizona, but a turn of events took me to Utah to finish the book. Although my daughter lives there, it was still unfamiliar territory. Along with temporary lodgings, I needed a kitchen that looked like the one I had been using in Arizona. My prayers were answered when my new friend, Sherry Young, said to me, "Use my kitchen, it's just what you are looking for!" After this, we found wonderful children to prepare the recipes for the photos. The children were always kind and welcoming. The parents and grandparents that brought their children were amazing. We had so much fun, like always, teaching recipes to the kids. Thanks to my daughter and to Sherry Young for making all the elements of the book come together. Once again, the power of prayer has been the lamp that lights my way. I hope this book can be a lamp of color to light the way for children to learn about food as they enjoy making these recipes.

A special thanks to my daughter, Ashley Wick Huffaker, who always helps me find perfect recipe preparers for the photos. I'm grateful that Ashley always knows what to say to the children to get the most amazing photos and cute smiles. She has a natural talent for photography that has brought this book to life.

A special thank you to Ellen Ohoro, who is an amazing assistant. She does much to assist others in doing good in the world. She provides me with honest feedback and encouragement for my projects.

Also thanks to my publisher, editor, and designer. They have been an amazing team.

ABOUT THE AUTHOR

Jacque grew up in Denver, Colorado. She loved living her young life as a cowgirl. Along with dance and music, she learned to trick rope and became Little Miss Colorado. When she was old enough to stand at the stove, she taught herself to cook. Instantly she loved the smells and creations that came along with cooking. After college she married her love of her life, an educator from Arizona. She then taught and worked with her husband at the family's school in Sedona, Arizona. While they lived on the school campus, she loved to prepare food for school parties and cookouts. Jacque's husband died unexpected at a young age. Being a young widow with a baby and a toddler, Jacque began to publish teaching material from her home. She was a pioneer in working from home for women during that time. Tutoring children, especially those with ADHD, has brought Jacque happiness throughout the years. She loves having adventures and meeting new people. Jacque enjoys spending time with her kids and recently new grandkids. She lives in Arizona and Utah with her little dog, Kanga.

FANS OF *COLORFUL COOKING*

"Jacque Wick has done it again with *Colorful Cooking*. Not only does she have yummy recipes that are easy for kids to follow, but she also inspires them to be creative in the kitchen. Her book gets parents and grandparents involved to create a great family bonding experience. A must have!"

JOLIE VANIER
Actress/Author

"Jacque Wick's *Colorful Cooking: Healthy and Fun Recipes Kids Can Make* is fantastic for teaching young children about food and cooking. Cooking is a skill that should be consistently taught in every home."

LIZ EDMONDS
The Food Nanny

"*Colorful Cooking* helps adults and kids learn the basics of the science behind foods' colors. Jacque Wick shows parents how to let kids' creativity flourish in the kitchen. Her recipes are kid friendly, and keep in mind all those picky eaters. Fantastic book!"

DR. DAVID CURRAN, M.D., F.A.A.P.
Department of Pediatric Medicine, Cardon Children's Medical Center

"I had the pleasure of watching as Jacque orchestrated the children's cooking while her daughter Ashley shot pictures of all the different steps. The cooking and filming in and of itself was impressive. Then Jacque sent me a preview of the book.

What a treasure it is, with so much information about nutrition and why it is fun and wise to eat colorful foods. The pictures and recipes should encourage positive interaction between parents and children, and will help even the pickiest of eaters enjoy some new foods. The book also makes an excellent gift for any occasion."

SHERRY YOUNG
Columnist for *Deseret News*, Salt Lake City, Utah

Child Chefs and Taste Testers

RED FOOD

STRAWBERRY SHORTCAKE CREPES: Ellie Erickson

FIESTA SALSA: Magdalene Jean Rogers (3)

CHOCOLATE STRAWBERRY DIPS: Stella Madsen (4)

MANGO BERRY SELTZER: Lillian Young (5)

ORANGE FOOD

CINNAMON SWEET POTATO FRIES: Jameson Huffaker (2)

ORANGE CHOCOLATE CHIP COOKIES: Ava Ernest (5)

BUNNY HOP FLOAT: Ellie Erickson

CREAMY ORANGE SYRUP: Sadie (5) and Mason (3) Sandstrom

YELLOW FOOD

READY SET GO CORN ON A STICK: Maisy Smith (2), and Mollie Smith (4)

FROZEN PINEAPPLE FLUFF: Jane Miller (6), and Nicklaus Miller (2)

BANANA SPLIT CUPS: Lillian Young (5)

GREEN FOOD

ZESTY EDAMAME: Jameson Huffaker (2)

FROSTY ZUCCHINI CUPCAKES: Jordan Ofahengaue

AWESOME AVOCADO SPREAD: Lyam Mortimer (1.5)

BLUE FOOD

GRAPE BERRY MUFFIN CUP: McKenzie Flake (5)

BLUEBERRY-LICIOUS PANCAKES: Sadie (5) and Mason (3) Sandstrom

BERRY SWIRL SLUSH: Josiah Austin (4), and Alayna Austin (6)

BROWN FOOD

SOY GOOD FRIED RICE: Jordan Ofghangaue

APPLE CRISP CUPS: Stella Madsen (4)

VANILLA WARM FUZZIES DRINK: McKenzie Flake (5)

DOUBLE TROUBLE DIRT SHAKE: Jameson Huffaker, (2) and Lyam Mortimer (1.5)

COLORFUL FOOD

COLORFUL TORTILLA WRAP: Isabel Christensen (3.5)

COLORFUL SASSY SALAD: Scarlett Noelle Cook (5)

COLORFUL WAFFLE QUESADILLA: Magdalene Jean Rodgers (3) Jameson Huffaker (2)

COLORFUL MAC AND CHEESE: Ayla Burnham (6)

JUL 2 8 2015